# CONTENTS

PAGE

INTRODUCTION                                          3

PART 1   -   Life

    1.   *The Human Image*                          7
    2.   *Life in Our Hands*                         18
    3.   *Force and Violence*                        28
    4.   *The Peace Movement*                        38


PART 2   -   Love

    5.   *Love Minus Zero*                           49
    6.   *The Power of Love*                         60
    7.   *Love Minus*                                72
    8.   *Throwaway Relationships*                   83


PART 3   -   Liberty

    9.   *Christian Liberation*                      97
    10.  *Freedom from Addiction*                   108
    11.  *Chimes of Freedom*                        120
    12.  *Future Freedom*                           135

To my father
- the shepherd who sang
for the lost sheep

# INTRODUCTION

This book is about the necessity of Christian belief. In particular, it is about the relevance of Christianity to various areas of moral and personal dilemma. Twenty years ago, as a student in Edinburgh, I felt an increasing sense of bewilderment, as I tried to see how Christianity related to the real world. The prevalent attitude was 'Christianity - who needs it?' But then, through the writings of Francis Schaeffer, Hans Rookmaaker and C.S. Lewis, I made the great discoveries that Christianity is true and Christ is the Lord of the whole of life. Over the years since then I have come to see that Christianity is exactly what the world needs.

I suggest that we have three great needs. We need to know the origin and value of human life. We need to know the origin and the rules of love. And we need true freedom. These are the three areas considered in this book - life, love and liberty. Of these, love is central because, as one has said of another triad, 'the greatest of these is love', hence the title 'Love Minus Zero'.

It may seem to the reader that as I look at these areas I mix three approaches - the theological, the ethical and the evangelistic. This is not accidental. I believe it is a mistake that these approaches are too often divorced. After all, if Christian theology is true, then it has ethical and evangelistic consequences. It does not just affect what you believe, but what you do as well. And if you want to communicate the good news of Jesus Christ effectively to sinners, then you must be able to show what kind of contemporary behaviour is sinful, you must be aware of people's moral standards and sense of moral failure, and you must be able to explain clearly what Christian doctrine is. Equally, if you wish to promote Christian ethical standards in our society, the attempt will fail miserably unless linked closely with the presentation of Christian truth and its implications. If told to be good, many people today will ask 'Why?' The doctrines of the gospel provide the answer. To my mind theology, ethics and evangelism are inseparable.

Thanks are due to various people. I originally prepared most of the material used in Chapters 1 and 2 for a report of the Study Panel of the Free Church of Scotland entitled *The Sanctity of Human Life*. I wish to express my gratitude to the late Dr N.A.R. Mackay and other members of the Study Panel for their helpful criticism and for their permission to use that material in this book. In particular I wish to thank Mr Colin Mackay, consultant surgeon, for permission to use material he prepared on euthanasia. It should go without saying that any shortcomings are my own responsibility. Also, a lot of the material of Chapters 3 and 4 was given in a talk entitled 'The Christian Response to the Peace Movement' at the 1987 Free Church School in Theology and later appeared under the same title in *The Reformed Theological Journal*. In addition, the material of Chapter 10 first appeared in serial form in *The Instructor,* the youth magazine of the Free Church of Scotland.

Thanks to Colin Morison and Kathleen Maciver of Christian Focus Publications for their unfailing courtesy, patience and encouragement. A special word of thanks to James Beaton who was foolhardy enough to ask me to start writing this book in the first place and to the Kirk Session of Bon Accord Free Church for giving me time off to finish it.

Above all I want to thank my wife, Evelyn, and four children, Katharine, Douglas, Alison and Robert for their understanding and support when I disappeared into the study even more than usual!

# PART 1

# LIFE

CHAPTER 1
# THE HUMAN IMAGE

Recent developments in medical science affect human life in an unprecedented way. Indeed, they raise the fundamental question as to what is human life. These developments, which tend to cluster around the beginning and the end of life, include Artificial Insemination, In Vitro Fertilisation, Egg Donation, Embryo Donation, Surrogacy, Embryo Experimentation, Birth Control, Abortion, Postnatal Treatment, Transplantation and Euthanasia.

These techniques raise specific moral problems and these will be looked at in Chapter 2. But as most of them raise the basic questions of the value of human life and what life may be described as human life, I wish to deal with these questions first.

## *The Value of Human Life*

Has human life any special value? The answer depends on one's philosophy or explanation of the universe. And there are only two serious alternatives. Either the universe is explicable in personal terms (it was created and is being sustained by God) or it may be explained in impersonal terms by some naturalistic, mechanistic or evolutionary theory. It is strange that there is no generally recognised term to describe this latter position, as it forms the intellectual furniture of our generation. I call it impersonalism.

Impersonalism holds that human life is only the product of millions of years of the chance development of matter. All existence is an uninterrupted continuum from the hydrogen atom to the human brain. All life is an uninterrupted continuum from the amoeba to man. There was, and is, no Intelligence outside the universe to create it and sustain it. The astronomer Fred Hoyle puts it like this:

'Only the biological processes of mutation and natural selection are needed to produce living creatures as we

know them. Such creatures are no more than inge-
nious machines that have evolved as strange by-prod-
ucts in an odd corner of the Universe . . . . Most people
object to this argument for the not very good reason
that they do not like to think of themselves as
machines'.[1]

Psychologist B.F. Skinner agrees: 'Man is a machine in the
sense that he is a complex system behaving in lawful
ways'.[2] But not only is man merely a machine, according
to this view, he is also a machine produced merely by
chance. Jacques Monod, the molecular biologist, expresses it in popular terms: 'The universe was not pregnant
with life nor the biosphere with man. Our number came
up in a Monte Carlo game'.[3]

## The difficulties of impersonalism

However, impersonalism involves two insuperable difficulties. The first concerns its reliability, the second its consequences. The first difficulty is what C.S. Lewis called
'the cardinal difficulty of naturalism'. He quotes Professor
Haldane:

'If my mental processes are determined wholly by the
motions of atoms in my brain, I have no reason to sup-
pose that my beliefs are true . . . and hence I have no
reason for supposing my brain to be composed of
atoms'.[4]

C.S. Lewis himself describes this difficulty of naturalism in
these terms: 'It offers what professes to be a full account
of our mental behaviour; but this account, on inspection,
leaves no room for the acts of knowing or insight on
which the whole value of our thinking, as a means to
truth, depends'.[5] In other words, there is no basis for the
validity of human reasoning in impersonalism.

The second difficulty is that if impersonalism is true,
then it is impossible to introduce any notion of the inher-
ent value of any part of the universe over other parts.
Particularly, if the evolutionary process has resulted in the
emergence of a being with greed and cruelty enough to

destroy the whole of his and other species' environments, how can it reasonably be argued that he is higher than other species and not lower?

The truth is that there can be no basis in any form of impersonalism for the belief that human life has an intrinsic value greater than that of a blue whale, a rabbit, or even a fly. Any sentimental feelings for the value of human life must be purely irrational. Indeed the compassion that desires to protect and save even the weakest human individual must, in evolutionary terms, be deemed counter-productive, as one of the foundations of evolutionary theory is the principle of natural selection (the survival of the fittest).

It is no coincidence, after some form of impersonalism being taught in our schools, universities and medical colleges throughout this century, that we now have some members of the medical profession who give strong support to abortion, euthanasia and experimentation on human embryos. Nor was it any coincidence that it was in Nazi Germany (shaped by an amalgum of Hegelian philosophy and Darwinian theory) that the medical profession co-operated in the mass extermination of the chronically sick and of those considered socially disturbing or racially and ideologically unwanted. The plain fact is that there is no basis for the value, dignity and sanctity of human life in any form of impersonalism.

## *The Christian basis*

If there is no basis there, is there a basis anywhere? I am convinced that Biblical Christianity provides the only firm basis for belief in the value of human life. The relevant doctrines are - the existence of the unlimited but personal God who has created the world and revealed himself in the Scriptures, and the creation of man in the image of God.

Once we know that the ultimate reality of the universe is not the Impersonal, the matter or energy of which it is made, but the Personal, the Creator who made it, then we immediately have a basis for the worth of man and the sanctity of his life. The Bible spells it out. Man is not the end product of the purely blind and random combination of atoms. He has been created by God as the only personal creature that inhabits the material universe. He is described as being in the image of God (Genesis 1:26,27; 9:6; 1. Corinthians 11:7; James 3:9), a description that does not cease to be true after the Fall, as three of the above references are to man in his post-Fall condition. It is true that sin has marred that image. Holiness, righteousness and knowledge have been lost, and these can only be restored in Christ (Ephesians 4:24; Colossians 3:10). However, it is clear from Genesis 9:6, 1 Corinthians 11:7 and James 3:9 that man in his sinful, fallen condition still bears the image of God in some way. Theologians may disagree as to the exact import of that description, but the Biblical description cannot be denied.

## *The image of God*

The best way of understanding the expression, 'the image of God', is to interpret it in the light of the context in which it was first revealed (Genesis 1:26-30). Man's likeness to God is linked with man's rule over the earth. Indeed it can be said that it is in his ability to rule and have dominion over other creatures that his God-likeness is expressed. The image of God is expressed in all the abilities that distinguish man from the animals and equip him to rule over them.

Our Lord Jesus also taught that the worth of man is linked to his superiority over animals. He said, 'How much more valuable is a man than a sheep!' (Matthew 12:12, NIV). However, it must be said that, although a man may lose some or all of the abilities which distinguish him from the animal, he does not cease to be a man nor does he become an animal. The very man of whom Jesus was speaking was a handicapped person. He had a withered hand. Even in his severe handicap he still differed from the sheep. Whereas the sheep could never have the creative potential of a hand, the man could, if it was restored. It is precisely in this way that we must view the difficult cases. No matter how poor, weak, handi-capped or demented a human being becomes, he never descends to the status of an animal, because, unlike the animal, he can be restored, if not by the power of man, then by the power of God; if not in this life, then in the life to come.

It is better to say, therefore, that the image of God is *expressed* in man's God-like abilities, rather than it *con-sists* of these abilities. Among these abilities are - (1) the managerial ability to rule over the earth (Genesis 1:28), (2) the creative ability to rationally re-order the environ-ment (Adam was placed in a garden to work it, Genesis 2:15), (3) the scientific ability to describe and catalogue the other creatures (Genesis 2:19,20) and (4) the personal ability to relate to, communicate with and love another person (God, and also Eve, Genesis 2:22-25). Man's life has meaning, dignity and value, because he is related, on the level of personal being, to the God who created him. The Creator has endued man with the God-like qualities of rational thought, creativity and speech, he has crowned him with glory and honour, and he is pleased to declare that man is made in his image.

## *Divine protection*

It is this doctrine of the image of God that is made the basis for God's protection of human life. Murder is seen as such a heinous crime precisely because it strikes at what is most God-like in this world - a human being (see Genesis 9:6). It is this passage too that gives us the distinc-tion between lawful and unlawful killing. The only lawful taking of human life is the retributive execution of one guilty of murder (and, by extension, the waging of a just war). The taking of *innocent* human life is always con-demned in the Scriptures.

However, it is not only the deliberate taking of human life that is condemned, but also the deliberate neglect to save life. This is one of the main points of the story of the Good Samaritan. The question at issue was the law's requirement to love one's neighbour (the second great commandment, which sums up our duty to our fellow man). The priest and the Levite clearly broke the law of God by leaving the man to die. The particular aspect they were neglecting was the positive duty involved in the sixth commandment. Jesus was teaching that to allow a person to die, when one has the means to restore him to life, is as reprehensible as murder.

The question as to whether human life has any special value is answered affirmatively by the Christian. Human life is created in the image of God and protected by divine sanction.

## Which beings are human beings?

Our first question was primarily a philosophical/theological one; our second is primarily a biological one. The question of which beings are human beings, or what life may be described as human life, is fundamentally biological in nature. Nevertheless, there are relevant biblical data to be considered also, and these will be dealt with first.

## The Biblical Data

The first relevant biblical emphasis is the body-soul unity of the human person. This unity is evident in the creation of man (Genesis 2:7), in the consequences of the Fall being physical as well as spiritual (Genesis 3:16-19) and in the New Testament doctrine of the resurrection. However, we need look only at the first of these. When God created man, physical life and psychological life came into existence simultaneously. As soon as man was living, he was a living soul. A practical application of this is that, if it can be shown that an embryo or fetus is a living human body, the presumption must be that it is also a living human soul.

But how is pre-natal life in particular viewed in biblical

thought? There are several points to be considered here. In the first place, throughout the Bible the baby in the womb is assumed to be a living human being. The normal post-natal words are used to describe him - *child, babe, son* (Genesis 25:22, Exodus 21:22, Luke 1:44 etc.). Prenatal life is described as part of one's own personal history (Psalm 139:13-16) even from the point of conception (Psalm 51:5). In addition, the term *beget* is used throughout the Scriptures of the father's role in the procreation of his child. Both the Hebrew and Greek words mean to *bring forth*, to *bring into being*, to *generate*. Now the only role the father has in the conception of the child is in fertilisation. He provides the seed that fertilises the woman's egg. This clearly implies that fertilisation, as a result of the procreative act, brings a new human being into existence.

In the New Testament, 'sorceries' (*pharmakeia*) is listed among the works of the flesh (Galatians 5:20), and 'sorcerers' (*pharmakoi*) are among those excluded from the New Jerusalem (Revelation 21:8, 22:15). The *pharmakoi* were medicine men or witch doctors and one of their important functions in the ancient world was the provision of abortifacient drugs. In the Revelation passages the sorcerers are linked with fornicators and homicides, and this would support the view that it is particularly the abortion activities of the *pharmakoi* that are in mind, as fornication was (and is) a frequent reason for abortion, and also, early Christians and Jews identified abortion with homicide (see *The Didache*, and Josephus, *Contra Apion 2:202, Antiquities 4:277*).[6]

The only biblical passage that has ever been thought of as taking a different view of pre-natal life is Exodus 21:22-25. But a careful exegesis reveals that this is not the case (see, for instance, Calvin's Commentary). The crucial part reads literally, 'If men fight and they strike a pregnant woman and they cause her child to come out and there is no serious injury . . .' There is no indication at this point that the child is born dead rather than simply early. Nor is there any indication that the 'serious injury' refers only to the woman and not to the child also. The natural reading of v.22 is that if the child is born alive and well, the culprit is fined, whereas in the case of the death or injury of the child or mother, the normal penalty for murder or assault is stipulated (vs. 23 and 24). Thus, far from lowering the status of pre-natal life, this passage clarifies that it has equal status with post-natal life.

However, it is the incarnation which gives us the strongest reason for holding that pre-natal life is human life. The argument may be presented as follows. For fundamental theological reasons it is necessary that Christ is fully human (see Hebrews 2:14-17). Christ's human life began at conception in the womb (literally 'in the belly') of the virgin Mary (Matthew 1:20 and Luke 1:31). Therefore, human life must begin at conception. (It ought to be noted here that, until extremely recently, conception was always understood to be fertilisation. But on this, see below, under *The Biological Data*).

Important as all these biblical emphases are, they are not essential to the case which I am arguing. Once it has been established that human life has special value and divine protection, the question as to what constitutes human life can be answered biologically.

## *The Biological Data*

A fundamental of biological science is that natural life begins at fertilisation with the irreversible union of the nuclei of the sperm and ovum to form the zygote (or one-cell embryo) which has the whole genetic code to spell out the characteristics of this new individual. Thus, if we were able to 'read' this code in a human embryo, we would know the sex, the colour of eyes, hair and skin, the facial features, the body type and certain qualities of personality and intelligence of this individual human being.

In biological terms, the one-cell embryo is a living human individual. It has the basic attributes of *life* (growth and reproduction). It is a distinctively *human* organism. And it is a *whole, individual organism* (as distinct from part of one). Therefore, we must conclude that the one-cell embryo is a living human organism (or body). And the presumption, in Christian terms, is that where there is a living human body, there is a living human soul.

It must be stressed at this point that there is a difference between the one-cell embryo, on the one hand, and the sperm and ovum, on the other, which is almost impossible to exaggerate. Neither the sperm nor the ovum is a whole individual human being. Each has only half the necessary genetic material, and is not capable of self-reproduction. No characteristics of a human person can be attributed to it. For instance it cannot be said whether it constitutes a male or female person, because that is only determined by the formation of the zygote. The only point in the development of a human being, at which there is a distinct discontinuity with what went before, is fertilisation.

However, because this position is judged to create serious difficulty especially for medical scientists working in embryo research, it is argued that there are other stages in the development of the embryo at which it becomes a human being or person. The two stages most commonly argued for are implantation and the formation of the central nervous system.

Those who favour implantation as the point at which human life begins, argue that there is a serious objection to the view that life begins at fertilisation. It is estimated that large numbers of embryos do not survive because they do not implant in the womb. (It ought to be remembered that these estimates may be wrong). It is also thought that many of these embryos may be abnormal in some way. From this it is deduced that human life cannot begin until implantation, because we cannot accept such wastage of human life. This does not at all follow. We may find such loss of human life unacceptable, but that does not prove that it does not occur. At one time the infant mortality rate was unacceptable, but the deduction was not made that infants are not human. In addition, it must be pointed out that, however marvellous the process of implantation is, it appears to be simply the means whereby the already complex embryo is provided with feeding and a friendly environment. If it does not have these, it will die, in the same way in which any human being will die, if deprived of food and shelter.

It is also argued that, since we now define the end of life in terms of brain death, we should define the beginning of life in terms of the formation of the central nervous system. This sounds attractive and plausible, especially in light of the fact that neurons are the only cells in our bodies that are irreplaceable. When the neuron dies it is not replaced. However, it is quite easy to see the discontinuity between a living neuron and a dead one. It is not at all easy to see a similar discontinuity between a living neuron and the living ectodermal cell from which it developed. The nucleus of every neuron has an exact copy of the genetic code which came into existance at fertilisation, so there is a distinct continuity back to that point. Fertilisation is the beginning of life, just as irreversible brain death is its end.

Later stages of fetal development have been urged as points when life may be said to begin. The most common of these are viability (the capability of living outside the womb) and birth itself. In reality this is a single argument and it has no biological basis whatsoever. The main difference is that the baby outside the womb receives oxygen through its lungs, while the baby inside the womb receives oxygen through his umbilical cord from his mother - hardly a difference between life and non-life.

However, even if there were uncertainty about the status of the embryo, then logically we must afford it full protection. Of course the opposite has been argued - 'The embryo may not be a person, therefore we owe it no protection'. But would we suggest, in the case of a mountain-rescue operation, 'Call it off, they may be dead?' Or would we approve of a demolition firm who blew up a building and said, 'We don't know if there are people inside or not?' Where the possible presence of human life is concerned, doubt is not an adequate basis for withdrawal of protection. In our context, the burden of proof lies on those who argue that the embryo is not a human being. Unless they prove their case, we can take no liberties, because, if we are unsure of the status of the embryo, killing it may be morally no different from killing a child.

CHAPTER 2
# LIFE IN OUR HANDS

We live in an age when medical science has made huge advances from which we have all benefited. The medical profession has won enormous respect, and rightly so. It is also widely recognised that Christianity has played a vital role in the birth and progress of modern medicine in the western world. Nevertheless, as we come to consider some areas of medical development, we see that medicine is not immune to the pressures caused by the moral vacuum left by the replacement of Christianity with impersonalism in our society. Rather medicine has become the testing ground of new ideas with regard to the value of human life and other areas such as marriage. No longer is there consensus on the basis of Christian absolute values. No longer is there confidence that human life and marriage are sacred. Instead, various relative values are weighed against one another. Life and marriage are seen as only two relative values among others more vague, such as compassion, or more potentially sinister, such as social progress.

We come now to look, in the light of Christian principles, at the various areas of medical development which were mentioned at the beginning of Chapter 1. As we do so, we must bear in mind that contrary arguments are put forward by others in the name of such values as 'compassion'. But we must recognise that there is no basis for compassion in impersonalism. If man is merely a machine, compassion (along with every other value) is meaningless. We are back in the nightmare world of Nazi Germany where words could mean anything, where *The Charitable Transport Company for the Sick* was the agency for conveying people to the extermination centres. There is a basis for compassion only in the Christian ethic, and in any particular instance we must ask whether the action demanded in the name of 'compassion' violates a clear principle of Christian morality. For instance, it is right and Christian that we should be compassionate to infertile couples, to unmarried expectant mothers and to the terminally ill, but such compassion cannot advocate actions which violate the commands of the God of compassion. (For more on the interface of love and the moral law see Chapter 5).

## Artificial Insemination

The term 'artificial insemination' is used to refer to the placing of semen inside a woman's body by means other than sexual intercourse. It is the simplest technique used for the alleviation of infertility. Neither artificial insemination by husband (AIH) nor artificial insemination by donor (AID) raises the question of the sanctity of life, as, obviously, AI takes place before fertilisation. However, AID raises another ethical problem. Does the use of the sperm of another man constitute an infringement of the exclusive unity of marriage as the Biblical law? While it is not clear that AID involves an adulterous act *per se*, I think that the intrusion of a third party does constitute an invasion of the exclusive unity of marriage, involved in the positive ethical principle, 'A man shall leave his father and mother and be united to his wife and the two will become one flesh' (Matthew 19:5).

This position was confirmed by the Warnock Report in its recognition that the children born as a result of AID are illegitimate under present law.[1] Of course, the recommendation of Warnock was that the law should be changed. However, there is very good reason for the law relating to illegitimacy. It protects the status of marriage and the children of a marriage. The changes envisaged by Warnock would involve legal falsehoods; for instance, in the entry of the name of a man as father who is not the father of the child. They would also involve, in certain circumstances, some children having no father at all in the eyes of the law.

## *In Vitro Fertilisation*

Although a complex medical procedure, IVF basically differs from natural fertilisation only in that it takes place outside the woman's body. This technique is relevant when a woman can produce healthy eggs, but owing to blocked fallopian tubes, the egg cannot pass from the ovary to the uterus. There is nothing inherently wrong with IVF provided that (a) it is performed for the purpose of treating infertility, (b) the ovum and sperm come from a married couple, (c) the resultant embryo(s) are placed in the wife's uterus, and (d) there is no destruction of, or experimentation on 'spare' embryos. Provisions (a), (b) and (c) are primarily to safeguard the sanctity of the marriage bond and the well-being of any children born, whereas (d) concerns the sanctity of human life. If, as I have attempted to show in Chapter 1, human life must be afforded full protection from fertilisation onwards, it is particularly reprehensible to destroy the defenceless human embryo. (On the question of embryo experimentation, see below).

## *Egg Donation, Embryo Donation and Surrogacy*

These techniques are advocated where it is the wife who is infertile (or sometimes both partners). They also may involve in vitro fertilisation and/or artificial insemination (see above). Although in terms of medical complexity these techniques differ widely from AID, in ethical terms they are similar, because they also involve the intrusion of a third party (in this case a woman) into the married relationship. Egg donation involves the recovery of an egg from a fertile woman donor, which is fertilised in vitro using the semen of the patient's husband and then transferred to the uterus of the infertile patient. The main difference with embryo donation is that there it is usually the semen of a donor that is used, instead of the husband's semen.

Surrogacy is the practice whereby one woman carries a child for another with the intention that the child should be handed over after birth. Of these techniques, it is only surrogacy that Warnock, rather inconsistently, was prepared to outlaw.[2] (But, of course, Warnock is taking its stand not on a coherent set of ethical principles but upon what is deemed to be socially expedient). In my view, all of these techniques are open to the fatal objection that they intrude a third party into the married relationship, and that at the most intimate point of the procreation of children.

## Embryo Experimentation

By embryo experimentation is meant procedures which may be carried out on the embryo, not for the good of the embryo (and in all likelihood for its harm and destruction), but for the supposed good of others or of society. These procedures may range from the testing of drugs on embryos to the production of 'carbon copy clones' for the provision of organs for transplantation. However, no medical procedure should be carried out upon the embryo that does not have as its aim the health of the embryo. As he is a living human individual, he must not be treated as a means to the end of the health or well-being of others. He must always be treated as the doctor's patient.

## Birth Control

I choose the term *birth control* quite deliberately in preference to contraception in this context, as it includes some measures which are not contraceptive (in the true sense of preventing fertilisation). The purpose of any method of birth control is, by definition, to control the number of children that are born. Apart from the question of the ethics of specific forms of birth control (see below), we must first consider the legitimacy of the purpose of birth control. Although the command of God to man is to be fruitful and multiply and fill the earth, there is no indication in the Bible that man is to go on multiplying once he has filled the earth. Rather, with limited resources, it would appear to be right to limit population growth. In addition there may be special reasons for limiting the size of a family, such as the wife's health, the risk of congenital abnormality or economic reasons (we are required to provide for our own families). It may be argued by some that in such circumstances it is abstinence that is required, not contraception. But in the light of the important role given by the Scriptures to sexual intercourse within marriage, irrespective of conception, abstinence cannot be the norm (see Genesis 2:24, 1 Corinthians 7:1-5.) Still, 'children are God's heritage', and the Christian in particular should not use contraception for purely selfish or materialistic reasons.

Certain methods of birth control are not true contraceptives at all, in that they act after fertilisation by preventing the implantation of the embryo in the uterus, thus causing its premature death. In this category are the 'morning-after pill'(which must be distinguished from the normal contraceptive pill which is intended to be a true contraceptive) and the intra-uterine device (IUD) or coil. This was known as the intra-uterine contraceptive device (IUCD) when it was first brought out in the USA, but it was soon recognised that it was not a true contraceptive. It too prevents the implantation of the embryo, although it is not known exactly how it does this. If we accept that the embryo is a living human individual from fertilisation, or even if we believe we must give it the benefit of the doubt, such birth control methods are unacceptable. While I recognise that a considerable number of women may have been using the IUD in ignorance of its exact effect, and therefore ought not to be condemned for that, yet, in the interests of the sanctity of human life and in honesty, I believe that the use of both the IUD and the 'morning-after pill'should be discouraged.

## *Abortion*

This is one of the few areas among those under discussion where there clearly is a present legal position. But this is often misunderstood or misrepresented. The fact is that abortion is still a criminal offence unless it is authorised by Section 1 of the Abortion Act 1967. This means, in summary, that abortion is an offence unless it is carried out by a registered medical practitioner in a N.H.S hospital (or other approved place) and that two medical practitioners have formed the opinion in good faith, either, that the balance of risk to the woman or her existing children as between termination and continuance of the pregnancy favours termination, or, that there is a substantial risk that the child would be born seriously handicapped. The above requirements concerning two doctors and 'approved places' do not apply if a doctor is convinced that termination is immediately necessary to save the life or to prevent grave permanent injury to the physical or mental health of the woman. (Such cases are, of course, extremely rare). It also appears that under Scottish law the offence of abortion may be committed at any stage between conception and birth, but there is no definite time limit for permitted abortions, as in England, where, under the 1929 Infant Life Preservation Act, the limit is 28 weeks, or earlier, if the child is capable of being born alive.

The 1967 Abortion act is extremely unsatisfactory, mainly because it takes no account of the human life of the fetus. If, as I believe I have shown, the destruction of the human embryo is contrary to the Christian ethic, how much more the destruction of a twelve week old fetus! By that stage of his development he has many of the recognisable characteristics of a human person. His heart has been beating for nine weeks, his brain activity has been detectable for six weeks, his unique fingerprints are already formed and he recoils from pain. Yet this is the living human individual whose little body is commonly torn apart by vacuum aspiration or dilation and currettage

(D&C) techniques. By later stages of pregnancy, when prostaglandin or hysterotomy techniques are employed, the fetus is, of course, even more highly developed and may even be born alive, unless poisoned or killed by some other direct act.

We must recognise, however, that there are very distressing cases involving very real moral, emotional or social dilemmas, where abortion is considered as a justifiable option. These are cases where a pregnancy threatens the life of the mother, is the result of the crime of rape or involves a handicapped fetus. On the basis of the Christian view of the sanctity of life there is clear support for the termination of a pregnancy where there is danger to the life of the mother, but as this normally happens late in pregnancy, it should in fact be a termination of pregnancy, not a termination of the life of the fetus. Everything possible should be done to save the life of the delivered baby.

While abhorring the crime of rape and expressing our sympathy and practical support to the victim, we cannot justify the abortion of the resultant embryo or fetus. Two wrongs do not make a right. The grievous harm already done to the woman will not be undone by an abortion. And, after all, the child conceived is her child too.

Advances in medical science have now made it possible to diagnose abnormalities in a child before it is born with the intention of offering abortion to the mother. This is euphemistically called 'prevention of handicap'. Unfortunately, the elimination of the handicap in this case also involves the elimination of the handicapped person. While in no way wishing to minimise the difficulties for a handicapped child and his family, we cannot condone abortion as the solution. It is for such 'elimination' that the name of the Nazis is still execrated today. In Christian thinking it is precisely the weak and the handicapped who most need care and protection.

## Post-natal Treatment

A most serious development in paediatrics in recent years has been the advocacy and practice by some paediatricians of allowing new-born children with birth defects to die (usually by sedation and non-feeding). It must be said that this is the logical outworking of the abortion mentality. 'If we already kill the baby in the womb, why not after he is born?' This is the end product of the application of relativistic impersonalism to medical ethics. Such neglect of the well-being of our needy fellow human being is exactly the kind of action deprecated by Jesus in the story of the Good Samaritan, and we as Christians must do all in our power to help the handicapped person.

## Euthanasia

It is not only in the area of the care of the new-born that death has been advocated as an option. It has also been urged as a 'treatment' for the terminally ill and the elderly. In this context, the term *euthanasia* is used to denote the deliberate termination of a person's life at the request of that person. At the present time, this is a criminal offence, in addition to being contrary to the law of God. However, there have been repeated attempts to change the law in order to give the individual the right of euthanasia. Although humanitarian reasons may be advanced for such a change, there are strong reasons against it.

Consider the situation which would arise should euthanasia be legalised. There would be great opportunity for the abuse of such a system by patients, relatives, friends and doctors. An elderly person who felt himself a burden to his family might think that he was obliged to request euthanasia, while inherently not desiring it. Relatives, wishing to be free of the responsibilities and restrictions of caring for an elderly person, friends, standing to benefit financially by a person's death, and doctors, seeing the problems of a person living on his own, might all encourage a person to request euthanasia.

Legalised euthanasia would also adversely affect the

medical profession. It would lead to distrust of doctors. The anthropologist Margaret Mead said that prior to the Hippocratic Oath people did not know if the doctor was coming as healer or killer. With euthanasia we would return to that situation. Elderly patients would become most reluctant to seek medical advice, fearing (albeit wrongly) that they might have their lives deliberately terminated. Thus, perfectly curable conditions might well go without treatment with fatal results. Medical practice would also decline. If a patient came to a doctor with some complaint and mentioned that they were not anxious to live, this might result in a failure on the part of the doctor to investigate the problem adequately and to administer the appropriate treatment.

There is also the fact that a person may change his mind. It is well established that people think differently under different circumstances. A person who wished euthanasia at one time of his life could later change his mind. It may be argued that there could be facilities for this to be done. But this would be impossible to administer properly, when the person involved was unable to express himself adequately, following a stroke, for instance.

There are some more technical medical points which should be mentioned in this connection. It should be recognised that it is wrong to use inappropriate medical measures to prolong the process of dying, and that it is equally wrong to deny sedation to the dying just in case there might be some respiratory depression. There should be adequate sedation without overdosage. The concept of brain death should also be recognised and, therefore, the principle of switching off the ventilator when patients are brain dead. The consequences of failing to do this would be that patients who suffer from correctable problems would not be able to get access to these ventilators, and so would die.

## *Transplantation*

Transplantation refers to the transfer of an organ or tissue from one individual to another. Blood transfusion is the most common form of transplantation. Blood containing living cells obtained from one individual is given to another individual. There is nothing inherently wrong with transplantation. Where problems appear to arise is with the use of cadaveric organs; that is, with the transfer of organs from a dead person to a living person. Provided that there are safeguards that the 'donor' is truly dead and that he (or his next-of-kin) has given permission for the transplantation of organs, there do not appear to be any biblical reasons why the transplantation of cadaveric organs should not be legitimate. Despite that, it must be said that there is something strangely schizophrenic about a society that aborts perfectly healthy babies, and at the same time spends millions of pounds in high prestige surgical programmes to prolong life for a few short months or years.

## *Medicine Men*

On the whole question of the sanctity of human life a choice confronts our society today. Are we to continue to have a Christian moral basis or not? If not, then let us at least be told whether it is to have a different moral basis or none. And if the desire is for no absolute ethic at all, it is clear we will be at the mercy of the powerful manipulators and conditioners so convincingly described by C.S. Lewis in *'The Abolition of Man'* and *'That Hideous Strength'*.[3] Are we to go ever further down the humanist road towards a neo-pagan society, where unwanted children are discarded and the new 'medicine men' dispense life or death for a fee, or are we going to draw back from the precipice and return to the Christian view of the dignity of man and the sanctity of human life?

CHAPTER 3
# FORCE AND VIOLENCE

Another attack upon the sanctity of human life comes from the apparently growing trend to violence, particularly in Western societies. If asked to diagnose what is wrong with the world, many people (perhaps the majority) would answer with one word - 'Violence'. Included in the connotations of the word would be everything from domestic violence to international war. We seem to have an instinctive abhorrence of the desecration of the human body by violence, yet violence persists and flourishes. Why is this? And why do some justify violence? Is there any connection between violence in the media and violence in real life? And is there any difference between violence and a legitimate use of force? These are some of the questions which I wish to examine in this chapter.

Why do we have the devastating phenomenon of violence, given its almost universal condemnation? There are three main explanations. We will call them, respectively, the ontological, the evolutionary and the moral theories of the origin of violence.

## *Violence simply is*

The ontological theory says that violence, like evil in general, is simply part of what exists. Violence is merely an aspect of man as man. Nobody can really be blamed for violence any more than he can be blamed for talking. This is a fundamental factor in today's 'no fault' morality. But it is not a new idea. It is an essential doctrine of all pantheism. For instance, in Hinduism, everything that exists is part of the One, or a manifestation of the One. And cruelty and death are represented by the goddess Kali, as one manifestation of reality. But if violence, cruelty and all evils are but aspects of the one ultimate reality, then there is no reason to oppose them, or even to say they are wrong.

The same dilemma is represented in a western context

by Albert Camus in *The Plague*.[1] The argument is presented against the background of an epidemic of the plague in the North African city of Oran. The view of the Roman Catholic Church (as perceived by Camus) is represented by the priest who believes that everything is equally God's will, including the plague. Therefore, it's wrong to fight the plague, as that would be fighting God's will. Camus' view is expressed by the doctor who chooses to fight the plague although he has no rational basis for doing so. The dilemma, as presented by Camus, is either we must blindly and irrationally fight evil, or else just accept it as part of 'whatever will be, will be'. Either way, evil just is.

The trouble with every form of the ontological theory is that it provides no reason for opposing evil in general and violence in particular, nor does it give any hope of finding a cure, because, according to it, evil always has been, and as far as we know, always will be, part of man's humanity. The same criticisms can be levelled at the evolutionary theory, which is really only another form of the ontological theory.

## Evolutionary Theory

According to the evolutionary theory, violence is a form of animal aggression which has got out of hand. Whereas intra-species aggression in the animal world is largely stylised and for defence of territory, in homo sapiens it has got inexplicably out of control. Some, like Arthur Koestler in *The Ghost in the Machine*, are essentially pessimistic: 'It appears highly probable that Homo sapiens is a biological freak, the result of some remarkable mistake in the evolutionary process'[2] and he closes the book with the words, 'Nature has let us down. God seems to have left the receiver off the hook, and time is running out'.[3]

Others, like Konrad Lorenz, are optimistic, but it is a blind optimism. In his book *On Aggression* he expresses confidence in 'the great constructors' of evolution to restore control.[4] Apart from the sleight of hand in introducing the connotation of personal control with the words 'the great constructors', when evolution is blindly impersonal, this view also ignores the fact that violence can be justified in terms of natural selection (the survival of the fittest) one of the pillars of evolutionary theory. If it is beneficial to the human species that the strong survive, and man is only an animal, then who can say that Adolf Hitler was wrong when he said, 'I cannot see why man should not be as cruel as nature?' And lest we think that an extreme view, Hitler's principle of 'might is right'is not much different from the opinion of U.S.A. Supreme Court Justice Oliver Wendell Holmes Jr., 'Truth is the majority vote of that nation that could lick all others'.[5]

However, as Dostoevsky pointed out last century in *The Brothers Karamazov*, it is a fallacy to equate human violence with animal aggression:

> 'People talk sometimes of bestial cruelty, but that's a great injustice and insult to the beasts; a beast can never be so cruel as a man, so artistically cruel. The tiger only tears and gnaws, that's all he can do. He would never think of nailing people by the ears, even if he were able to do it'.[6]

There is something so radically different about human violence that not only has evolutionary theory no cure, it does not even have a proper diagnosis.

## *A Cleansing Force?*

It will now have become apparent that not all believe violence is wrong. Some, as Os Guinness has shown in *The Dust of Death*, believe that violence is not so much a crisis in society as a catharsis, a constructive and cleansing power. He quotes Franz Fanon, spokesman for the Algerian revolution and the Third World, in *The Wretched of the Earth* as one of the most influential: 'Violence is a cleansing force. It frees the native from his inferiority complex and from his despair and inaction; it makes him fearless and restores his self-respect'.[7] This has become the thinking of many in the world today from Latin-

American liberationist priests to European Marxist terror-
ists.

Along similar lines, if set in a very different environment, was Lindsay Anderson's film *If*, the story of the
eruption of violence in an English boarding school. The
violent climax of the film, in which the boys shoot down
the headmaster and others with a machine gun, is justified
in terms of a cathartic rebellion against repressive authority. The problem with all such revolutionary concepts of
violence is that, in the modern absence of absolute justice
and law, they lead to a downward spiral of counterv io-
lence or to the setting up of a totalitarian régime even
more repressive than what it replaced (as in George
Orwell's *Animal Farm*).

## Media violence

This leads us to the important question of the role of the
media in the growth of violence in our society. Do films
like *If*, and others with much less artistic merit, promote,
discourage or merely reflect violence? The plea that violence in films, television and literature merely reflects a
violent society has always appeared to me to be a
specious one. First, it has been calculated that the average
American sees violence on television once every fourteen
minutes and a killing once every forty-five minutes. Now
America is a violent country, but if every American witnessed violence on that scale in real life, there would
soon be no Americans left to witness it! Second, I seriously doubt if it is the intent (it certainly is not the effect) of
any communication medium merely to reflect and not to
influence. Any portrayal of violent scenes is saying 'This is
bad', 'This is good' or 'This is just the way the world is'.
Either way, ideas are being communicated, opinions are
being influenced. But third, why are billions of pounds
spent on television advertising if television doesn't influence anyone?

We should draw a clear distinction between productions in which violence is condemned and productions in

which it is glorified or presented amorally; but, other things being equal, a covetous man who watches a lot of adverts is likely to become more covetous, a musical man who listens to a lot of music is likely to become more musical and a violent man who views a lot of violence is likely to become more violent. And this danger is compounded by the fact that there are violent tendencies in each one of us. If the twentieth century has convinced us of nothing else, it has surely convinced us of the fallacy of a Pelagian faith in the goodness of human nature. This is true not only of twentieth century history, but also of twentieth century art and literature. William Golding's *Lord of the Flies*, for instance, is a devastating exposé of the evil that lurks even in the most innocent and civilised. The boys, stranded on an island, create not a utopia, but a tyranny of violence and destruction.

## *The moral alternative*

What is the explanation of this deep-rooted violence? If the model of animal aggression fails (as I believe it does), is there any rational explanation? Or are we doomed to a dismal choice: either simply accept it as part of an absurd universe, or irrationally struggle against it, as Albert Camus urges in *The Rebel*? Is there any other alternative?

The alternative is the one from which all these others are trying to escape - that man's violence is part of his 'fallenness', his rebellion against his Creator, who made both him and his environment good. The philosopher C.E.M. Joad, who came to Christian belief after many years of agnosticism, says:

'It is because we rejected the doctrine of original sin that we on the Left were always being disappointed; disappointed by the refusal of people to be reasonable, by the subservience of intellect to emotion, by the failure of true socialism to arrive . . . . above all, by the recurrent fact of war'.[8]

The first murder is recorded in Genesis 4 - the murder of Abel by his brother Cain. But the first murder is inseparable from the first sin (in Genesis 3). The Fall of Adam and Eve leads on to the murder of one of their sons by the other. John Steinbeck in his novel *East of Eden* says: 'Two stories have haunted us and followed us from our beginning, the story of original sin and the story of Cain and Abel'.[9] Stuart Barton Babbage comments in his excellent book *The Mark of Cain*: 'It is these stories which provide the pattern for Steinbeck's exploration of the mystery of inherited guilt, of recurrent evil..... he is able to explore with extraordinary penetration the destructive ramifications of sin'.[10]

However, the Genesis account itself does more than explore, it provides us with the explanation of the origin of evil in general and of violence in particular. Human beings have not always been evil with violent tendencies. God saw all that he had made, including man, and declared it to be very good. And in the light of the fact that violence is everywhere condemned as evil in Scripture, it was obviously not part of man as he was created. That is the first indication of hope in the Christian position - violence is not part of man's essential humanity.

How then is the existence of violence explained? The biblical explanation is that violence (along with all evil) had an origin at a point in the history of the human race. That point we call the Fall, the point where man chose to disobey God and rebel against him. Therefore, the Christian explanation of evil is a moral one. Evil is not due to what man is essentially, but to what he has done, and what he has become as a result. In the case of Abel's murder, we see that the violent tendency of man is one of the miserable consequences of the Fall, the result of man's alienation from God, but also resulting in further alienation, as Cain is sent out from the presence of the Lord.

In addition, we see that in this moral explanation of evil there is hope. If evil is a disease, there is the possibility of a cure. If evil came by a man, then by a man evil may be destroyed. And also, Christianity does not have Camus' problem, as Francis Schaeffer pointed out in *The God Who is There*.[11] When we fight 'the plague' we are fighting not against God, but for God. He is irreversibly opposed to all evil and one day he will put an end to it. In the present he allows good and evil to coexist as he works out his purposes in history, but this means neither that he condones evil nor that he is impotent to prevent it, only that he is patient and longsuffering, giving men opportunity for repentance.

## Is killing always wrong?

One further point remains to be considered: is there a valid distinction between force and violence? Put bluntly, is killing always wrong? We live in an age of extremes and we are always in danger of moving from one extreme to the other. This is true concerning the sanctity of human life. In reaction to the tendency to undervalue human life there appears to be a growing emphasis upon a right to life without distinction. In an age that hates absolutes, the right to life might almost become a new absolute. Where there's life, there's a right to life! The question of guilt or innocence is not considered. No deed is considered so evil that the perpetrator ought to forfeit his right to life. Or even more sinisterly, exceptions to the absolute right to life are made, not on the basis of guilt or innocence, but on the basis of the presumed utilitarian value of a person to third parties or to society in general. It is thus that people with a generally high regard for human life justify the abortion of unplanned babies, and the euthanasia of handicapped newborn children or of the senile aged. And we have now the strange situation where the liberal establishment are anti-war, anti-force and anti-capital punishment, while simultaneously being pro-abortion!

What is the Christian alternative? Is it pro-life in the sense that all human life has an absolute right to life? No. The Bible is quite clear that the taking of human life is sometimes justified - in capital punishment and in the waging of a just war, for instance. But surely this is just as inconsistent as those who make exceptions for abortion! No, because in that case no moral guilt worthy of death can be attributed to the baby, whereas in this case, such guilt is precisely what is attributed to those meriting death. Let us look at the biblical data.

## A permanent sanction?

It is sometimes claimed that the principle of *Lex talionis* - 'a life for a life' - is restricted to the criminal law of Israel in the Old Testament, and because Israel as a theocracy ruled directly by God has come to an end with the New Testament, it is argued that this criminal law no longer applies. It is true that capital punishment is a prominent feature of the penal code of Israel, and that the theocracy has come to an end, but it is not as simple as that. The death penalty is first laid down long before the existence of Israel as a theocracy (in Genesis 9:6) and is reiterated in the New Testament (Romans 13:4) after the cessation of the theocracy.

The Genesis 9 passage is part of the covenant God made with Noah, and through Noah with the whole human race. Therefore, its stipulations (unless later changed or revoked by God) apply to all human beings. The relevant section reads -

'And from each man, too, I will demand an accounting for the life of his fellow man. Whoever sheds the blood of man, by man shall his blood be shed; for in the image of God has God made man' (Genesis 9:5,6).

The reference to the image of God not only gives the reason for the severity of the penalty, but also gives the basis for the administration of the just retribution. God is the ultimate judge, but because man is God's image he is also entitled to judge his fellow man. This is why rulers and judges are referred to as 'gods' in the Old Testament (for example, Psalm 82:6, a passage which Jesus quotes with approval in John 10:34,35, 'Scripture cannot be broken').

This position is re-emphasised in the New Testament. In Romans 13:1-7 the Apostle Paul deals with the role of civil authority or ruler -

'For he is God's servant to do you good. But if you do wrong, be afraid, for he does not bear the sword for

nothing. He is God's servant, an agent of wrath to
bring punishment on the wrongdoer' (Romans 13:4).
Therefore, it would appear that it is still God's decree in
the New Testament age that the civil authority should
have the power of capital punishment (of which the
sword was the symbol).

## Possible exceptions

However, there are three individual cases of murder
reported in the Bible which we must consider more closely, as they appear to be exceptions to the general rule. I
refer to the murders committed by Cain, David and Saul
of Tarsus. Cain's murder of his brother Abel does not create any serious difficulty for the view I have outlined, as it
took place before the Noahic covenant, and therefore in
an age when God was dealing with the human race in a
different way. It does prove that capital punishment is not
the only way God can choose to deal with murder, but
there is no evidence in the New Testament that we have
now returned to the pre-Noahic arrangements.

The other two cases are more problematical and have
some interesting light to shed on the question. Although
David did not kill Uriah personally (see 2 Samuel 11 and
12) yet it is clear that he procured his murder, and God
declared him guilty of murder (12:9). However, when
David confessed his sin, God declared that he would not
die - the death penalty was lifted (12:13). Nevertheless,
dire consequences followed in the judgement of God,
perhaps giving an indication that it is possible for the
death penalty to be commuted into some other appropriate penalty.

If this was possible under the old covenant with Israel,
it would appear that it is also possible under the new
covenant. Saul of Tarsus,too, was guilty of causing the
slaughter of innocent people (Acts 22:4, 26:10). No doubt
this was judicial murder, but it was murder nonetheless.
Nevertheless, God spared him and called him to a life of
Christian service as the apostle Paul. In fact it may be poss-

ible to view his lifetime's work as a reparation to the Church for the harm that he had done. There is evidence that Paul himself may have so viewed it (Galatians 1:23, Romans 1:14).

The Word of God teaches that the civil authority has the duty and power to punish the evildoer, even to the extent of executing the murderer. But it can be argued that a Christian civil authority also has, in certain circumstances, the duty and power to reflect the mercy of God by pardoning the offender or by commuting the sentence (as the Lord did in the cases of David and Paul). The question of where this might be appropriate is one over which Christians will no doubt disagree. And it must be borne in mind that the civil authority is primarily God's 'agent of wrath'.

However, it is clear that the Christian faith provides the necessary distinction between violence and the legitimate use of force. Violence is the violating of another's right to life (or other rights as in the cases of robbery or rape), but the civil authority has the right to restrain and punish evildoers, using force if necessary, and has the power to take the life of the murderer, who has forfeited his own right to life.

CHAPTER 4
# THE PEACE MOVEMENT

Peace is a great biblical concept, and therefore a great
Christian aspiration. The Messiah is the Prince of Peace,
his bequest to his disciples was peace and his ultimate
aim is to establish universal peace. So any movement
which advocates peace has an immediate emotional
appeal to the Christian. Indeed, in many circles the Peace
Movement is seen as a necessary outworking of
Christianity. But we must never forget that we live in an
age of connotation words, and being 'into peace'may not
be the same as being a peacemaker. Thus at the outset we
must ask, 'What is the Peace Movement? And why has it
developed?'

The Peace Movement is a very loose term describing
the development in the second half of the twentieth century of an anti-violence, anti-war stance among a considerable number of people. It is generally a heterogeneous
group ranging all the way from Buddhists to Mennonites,
and holding a variety of 'peace' views ranging from total
pacifism, through non-violent resistance, to nuclear pacifism.

As far as the Church is concerned, pacific views have
been represented throughout its history, witness
Tertullian, the Waldensians, the Anabaptists and the
Quakers. But until now it has tended to be the minority
view, except possibly among the early Fathers (the majority view being some form of the Just War Theory). But
why at this particular moment of history has there been
such an upsurge in pacifism?

There is a whole complex of reasons. First, there were
the two World Wars in the first half of the century. Not
only is there the sheer dismay at the destruction and dev-
astation, but also fear of what war does even to the vic-
tors. In an essay with the delightful title 'Blimpophobia',
named after the cartoon character Colonel Blimp and
written during the last war, C.S. Lewis pinpoints it with his

usual skill:

> 'We know from the experience of the last twenty years that a terrified and angry pacifism is one of the roads that lead to war. I am pointing out that hatred of those to whom war gives power over us is one of the roads to terrified and angry pacifism'.[1]

Second, ever since Hiroshima and Nagasaki, there has been the growing realisation of the horror of nuclear weapons. In 1958 Martin Luther King said, 'Today the choice is no longer between violence and non-violence. It is either non-violence or non-existence'.[2] And now there are the equivalent of 850,000 Hiroshima bombs, or over two tons of TNT for every man, woman and child on earth.

Third, there was the Protest and Civil Rights movement in the early Sixties, developing into the Vietnam Protests and Counter-Culture of the later Sixties and Seventies. Films like 'The War Game'and songs like Dylan's 'Masters of War'[3] and 'Hard Rain's gonna fall' influenced a generation.

Fourth, there is the growth of what may be called a superficial gospel. Many people conceive of Jesus as a Man of Peace and the Sermon on the Mount as his main teaching. This way of thinking cuts across all labels from Evangelical to Liberal.

## *Humanist Element in the Peace Movement*

Because there is such a variety in the peace movement, I think it is important for us to respond to the Christian element in it separately from what may be termed the humanist element. We have already seen in the previous chapter how humanism has no adequate explanation of the origin of violence nor does it provide any hope of a cure.

But of course the main emphasis of the Peace Movement is not just on violence in general, but on the possibility of a nuclear holocaust. That changes everything, we are told. But does it? As C.S. Lewis points out in an article '*On Living in an Atomic Age*'[4], one hundred per cent of us were already doomed to die before the invention of the Bomb, many of us in horrible ways. But it is insisted, what is new is that the Bomb may finally and totally destroy civilisation itself. 'The lights may be put out for ever'. But is that any different from what the secular humanist already believes about the world? Bertrand Russell wrote:

> 'That man is the product of causes which had no prevision of the end they were achieving; that his origin, his growth, his hopes and fears, his loves and beliefs, are but the outcome of chance collocations of atoms; that no fire, no heroism, no intensity of thought and feeling can preserve an individual life beyond the grave; that all the labour of the ages , all the devotion, all the inspiration, all the noonday brightness of human genius, are destined to extinction in the vast death of the solar system and that the whole temple of man's achievement must inevitably be buried beneath the debris of a universe in ruins - all these things, if not quite beyond dispute, are yet so nearly certain, that no philosophy which rejects them can hope to stand'.[5]

If both individual human beings and human civilisation are doomed to extinction anyway, why get excited about nuclear holocaust? And if on naturalistic presuppositions there is no basis for believing that human life is of any value anyway, why not rather push the button and end the whole miserable tragedy sooner rather than later?

## *Christian Pacificism*

We must now look at the case for pacifism put forward by Christians. There should be no dispute between Christian pacifists, on the one hand, and Christians who hold to the concepts of the legitimate use of force and the just war on the other, concerning the value of human life and the origin of violence, as outlined in previous chapters. It is specifically when we come to consider the question of the Christian's response to violence that Christian pacifists take their distinctive line.

They take as their foundation our Lord's words in the Sermon on the Mount, 'Do not resist an evil person . . . Love your enemies . . .' and in his non-retaliatory behaviour especially in the Garden and at Calvary. No matter what other passages of Scripture may say, their construction of this data is seen to be normative in formulating the Christian's response to violence. The Cross in particular is presented as God's way of dealing with violence. Jim Wallis contrasts the Cross and the Bomb:

'In the Cross, violence is defeated; in the Bomb violence is victorious. In the Cross, evil has been overcome; in the Bomb evil has dominion. In the Cross, death is swallowed up; in the Bomb death reigns supreme. Which will hold sway in our times?'[6]

Ronald Sider and Richard Taylor put it more carefully, if less poetically:

'The foundation of Christian non-violence lies not in some calculation of effectiveness. It rests in the Cross. The ultimate ground of biblical opposition to taking life is the nature of God revealed first in Jesus' teaching and life and then most fully in his death. If God in Christ reconciled his enemies by suffering servanthood, should not those who want to follow Christ also treat their enemies in the same way?'[7]

In other words, there is only one legitimate Christian response to violence - mercy, kindness and non-retaliation. And it is very difficult to see how, logically, on this principle, distinctions can be made between nuclear and conventional warfare and even the use of force by police or parents. Now I believe wholeheartedly that Jesus overcame the power of evil by his death and resurrection, but I also believe it is a logical and biblical non-sequitur to believe that individual conversion and the individual practice of non-violence is the only means whereby he will implement that victory in the world. All authority in heaven and earth is given to him. He is King of kings and, as we saw in the last chapter, they are his servants to punish evil.

## Participation in the State

Many Christian pacifists would allow a good deal of this, but would argue that participation in the state's activities is prohibited for the Christian. This is really an extraordinarily difficult position to maintain, without a shred of New Testament evidence to support it. Instead, in its pages we meet Christian soldiers and a Christian pro-consul, and we are exhorted to pray for and honour kings. How can we pray for them and honour them if what they are required to do is evil? How can we render to Caesar what is Caesar's, if what is Caesar's is evil? And if it is not evil, why is it not open to the Christian? In any case Paul tells us specifically the ruler is both 'God's servant to do you good' and 'God's servant, an agent of wrath'. Punishment of evil is doing good. And doing good is what Christians are commanded to do. Therefore, the Christian has a duty to participate in just government.

Certainly we must recognise the biblical emphasis on non-retaliation in personal matters. But does that mean that there is no place for justice? On the contrary, Paul says that in our refusal to take revenge we are leaving room for the wrath of God. And that does not refer only to the judgement of God in the life to come, for in the passage immediately following we are assured that the governing authority is an agent of God's wrath.

We must assert most emphatically that mercy and non-retaliation is not the only way God deals with evil in general and violence in particular. There will come a day when he will judge the world through Jesus Christ and he will sentence the wicked to hell, a second death far more horrific than mere physical death, a holocaust far more terrifying than the worst nuclear conflagration. And here and now he exercises judgement through the governing authorities. *He* resists the evil-doer. So resisting the evil-doer cannot be wrong absolutely.

## *War and Nuclear Weapons*

But finally I want to consider questions raised by war in general and nuclear war in particular. For many would say that modern warfare, and especially nuclear warfare, is irreconcilable with Christian principles, and that therefore we must at least be nuclear pacifists and urge unilateral nuclear disarmament. Let us consider war in biblical terms.

It is simply indisputable that God commanded Israel to wage war in the Old Testament period. These wars were always for just reasons. In the case of the Canaanites, it was because their sins were complete. Their gross wickedness, which included ritual prostitution and the religious sacrifice of children, called for total extermination. In other cases God stipulated that only the men were to be put to death. The women and children were to be spared. Other just wars were in self defence (as in Gideon's war with the Midianites and the various wars with the Philistines) or to defend a treaty partner against an aggressor (as in the case of Joshua's defence of the Gibeonites).

If war was not only allowed but commanded for Israel, how can it be disallowed for governing authorities in the New Testament age, who are agents of God's wrath punishing the evil-doer? In fact there is no such prohibition in the New Testament.

All this has, of course, led to the formulation over the centuries of what is known as the Just War Theory by such intellectual giants as Augustine and Hugo Grotius. War may be waged for just causes and by just methods. It is particularly in the area of method that we have problems today, especially with regard to avoidance of the killing of non-combatants. And the problems are not only with nuclear weapons. What about the firestorm bombing of Dresden in World War II? I believe purely civilian targets should not normally be attacked, but there may be circumstances in which non-combatants are killed because of the proximity of cities to military targets. There may also be occasions when the guilt of a nation is such that indiscriminate attacks may be justified, but only to prevent further crimes of the aggressor and to bring in a just peace, as was probably the *intention* in the case of the blanket bombing of German cities and the nuclear bombing of Hiroshima and Nagasaki.

We are now, of course, in a different situation. But it must be said that the difference of our situation does not lie in a new ability of man to kill millions of his fellow men. The Assyrians in the Middle East and Julius Caesar in Gaul managed that quite well with swords and spears. The difference lies in the fact that the superpowers confront each other in peacetime knowing they have the capability of mutual destruction. And that knowledge has kept the peace in Europe for over forty years. And it is only when both sides believe there is a military balance that there is stability and a desire to reduce the phenomenal costs by multilateral arms reduction. I believe we are seeing something of this at present. In contrast, the growth of what C.S. Lewis called 'a terrified and angry pacifism' in the Thirties was one of the roads to the Second World War. Hitler believed Britain would not go to war.

Further I do not believe that war or the credible threat of war is necessarily the worst alternative. Stalin killed twenty million of his fellow countrymen in peacetime in the 'Gulag Archipelago'. And twice as many people have been killed in Vietnam in the years since the war ended than were killed in the whole thirty years previously. Sometimes it is right to go to war or to threaten credibly to go to war in the cause of justice.

What about the specific strategies of nuclear defence? Are there problems there for the Christian? As I understand it, at the present time, nuclear deterrence defends Western Europe, not only against nuclear attack, but also against conventional attack. In other words it involves the 'first use' of nuclear weapons if Russian tanks rolled into West Germany (as they have rolled into Hungary, Czechoslovakia and Afganistan). Now it is often said that this is because it is cheaper to have a nuclear deterrent than the massive conventional forces required to repel a

Soviet attack. No doubt it is cheaper. But it is wrong to assume that by replacing nuclear deterrent with conventional deterrent we will be safe. As long as the USSR could back up conventional attack with nuclear attack, NATO forces would have to surrender. For the moment then we have to maintain our nuclear deterrent and be prepared to use it against conventional attack. And I believe it would be right so to use it.

To my mind there are only two safe alternatives. The first is the multilateral reduction of nuclear arms, such as is being negotiated at the present, but with the accompanying equalisation of conventional forces, which is just beginning to be considered at the time of writing. (Incidentally, it is most dishonest of the Peace Movement to claim these recent developments as a victory for their influence. If their viewpoint had been influential on the policies of the West, there would have been absolutely no reason for the USSR to come to the negotiating table. The two major reasons which caused the new reasonableness of the USSR were the strengthening of the West and the USSR's internal economic problems). The other alternative is the development by both sides of an adequate early-warning and interception system such as the 'Strategic Defence Initiative' which, in effect, renders nuclear weapons useless. This may be phenomenally expensive, but it may be the price we have to pay for a limited peace in a fallen world.

## Response to the Peace Movement

I believe we must respond to the Peace Movement by first of all carefully distinguishing between the humanist and Christian elements within it. To the humanist we must say that he has no basis for the value of human life in any case. And he has neither an adequate moral basis upon which to oppose violence nor a realistic hope of preventing it.

To our fellow Christian in the Peace Movement we must say that we agree with him about the value of human life and about the evil of violence, but we also believe that innocent human life is protected against the violence of the aggressor by the sanction of capital punishment and the just war. We believe in non-retaliation in individual matters, but we also believe that the Christian ruler has no right to turn other people's cheeks, rather he must defend them. If this is inconsistent, as the pacifist argues it is, then the inconsistency is not ours but Christ's, who did not retaliate to violence offered to him personally, but who as Messiah did cleanse the temple by force, and as King of kings will cleanse the universe in the day of the wrath of the Lamb.

Only two things remain to be said. First, there comes a time when the Christian must obey God rather than man. Not all wars declared by our country may be, or have been, right. We must refuse to take part in an unjust war. Second, although I disagree with the pacifist position and believe it to be profoundly dangerous in the present situation, I will defend the pacifist's freedom of conscience in the matter and would defend him from violence or unjust treatment by the state.

# PART 2

# LOVE

CHAPTER 5
# LOVE MINUS ZERO

One of the peculiarities of the human race is our obsession with love. It is difficult to think of a subject about which more ink has been spilt or more songs sung, or a phenomenon that has caused more extremes of happiness and despair. The Dylan who wrote the beautiful 'Love Minus Zero/No limit' later wrote the bitter 'Idiot Wind', probably about the same woman. The capacity to love and be loved is one of the most striking features of what Francis Schaeffer called 'the mannishness of man'. And in spite of all the hurt it has caused us, few of us would be prepared to change places with the animals.

But is love the tragedy of man? Are we always destined to have longings, impulses and desires that are ultimately unfulfillable? Are we for ever doomed to be disappointed in love, because no other human being can permanently satisfy us? Was it just a tragic mistake in the evolutionary process that produced human animals with this irrational and unquenchable desire? Food satisfies hunger, drink quenches thirst, even sexual desire is fulfilled in orgasm, but is there nothing in the universe that corresponds to my desire for love? Here only is there the mirage, never the oasis?

## God is Love

Into this bleak, twentieth century landscape there needs to come again the cascading torrents, the ocean depths and the mountain peaks of divine love. God is. And God is love. Man is not alone in an ultimately hostile universe. His longings to be completely understood, accepted and loved are totally fulfillable. His tragic (and blameworthy) mistake is in looking to his fellow human beings to be all-sufficient lovers. He worships and serves the creature instead of the Creator (Romans 1:25). Only God is the all-sufficient Lover. Love is not some grotesque mistake thrown up by the

blind impersonal process of evolution. Love is intrinsic to
the Originator of the universe. It has not arrived late on
the scene. It has always been there.

But this raises serious questions. If God is love, whom
could he love before he created the world? Was he lonely?
Was he unfulfilled? Did he need to create the universe in
order to love and be loved? This is where the Christian
doctrine of the Trinity is of staggering significance.
Judaism (in contra-distinction to Old Testament religion),
Islam and Unitarianism have no answers to these questions. The biblical, orthodox doctrine of the Trinity has.
For too long Christians have felt embarrassed and apolo-
getic about the Trinity. We must begin to realise that not
only does this doctrine do justice to the Biblical data, it
provides answers to some of the most problematic philo-
sophical, moral and religious questions of our age.

The Trinity is one of the radical doctrines of the
Christian faith which has been under constant attack in
the twentieth century, particularly in its emphasis on the
divinity of Jesus. So what is the doctine of the Trinity and
what is the evidence for it? The doctrine was hammered
out in the early Christian centuries in the face of heretical
deviations from apostolic doctrine, and is accepted by all
the major branches of the Church, Orthodox, Catholic and
Protestant. It is perhaps most succinctly stated in the
Westminster Confession:

'In the unity of the Godhead there be three persons, of
one substance, power and eternity; God the Father,
God the Son and God the Holy Ghost. The Father is of
none, neither begotten nor proceeding; the Son is eternally begotten of the Father; the Holy Ghost eternally
proceeding from the Father and the Son'.

## Oneness and Pluralness

What evidence is there for the Trinity? First there is the
biblical evidence. Throughout the Bible there are two
emphases: the oneness of God and the pluralness of God.
Or, in other words, the unity and diversity of the

Godhead. The Old Testament which uncompromisingly states the unity of God over against the polytheism of Egypt, Canaan and Babylon (Deuteronomy 6:4 etc.), also reveals the pluralness of God. The only living and true God who created the universe said, 'Let us make man in our image'. This plural cannot refer to any created beings (eg. angels), as only God is represented in Scripture as the Creator. It must refer to a pluralness within God. Similarly the very word for God in Hebrew (*Elohim*) is plural in form, although used with the singular form of the verb. In addition there is the person known as the Angel of the Lord. He comes from God, yet he is called the LORD (*Yahweh* or Jehovah) in Genesis 16:13. (Some other Old Testament passages to be considered are Psalm 45:6,7 and Isaiah 9:6).

It is, however, in the New Testament that the pluralness of God becomes apparent as trinity. First, there are the passages that show the deity of Jesus. The Word (Jesus) has always been God (John 1:1); he stated that he was eternally existing before the time of Abraham (John 8:58); he accepted the name of God of himself (John 20:28); he is God over all (Romans 9:5); he is in essential nature God (Phil. 2:6); he is our great God and Saviour (Titus 2:13). In addition to these quite explicit passages there are a whole host of passages which say things of Jesus which can only be true of God. He forgives sins which were committed against other men (Mark 2:5), which conduct C.S. Lewis described as 'asinine fatuity' unless he is God;[1] he claimed omnipresence (Matthew 18:20, 28:20); and he said he will judge the world (Matthew 25:31,32). From all this it is quite clear that Jesus and his apostles believed and taught that he is God.

Similarly, the Holy Spirit is described as God (Acts 5:3,4); he is omnipresent (Psalm 139:7-10); he was involved in the act of creation (Genesis 1:2); and he is the agent of the new birth (John 3:5,6). And, clearest of all, the Holy Spirit and the Son (and they only) are included with the Father in the one name of God (Matthew 28:19, see also 2 Corinthians 13:14).

God has always been love and God has always loved, because he is three: one God existing eternally as three persons, the Father, the Son and the Holy Spirit. Jesus, in speaking to the Father, said, 'You loved me before the creation of the world' (John 17:24). In the beginning the Word (Jesus) already was and he was always existing as God and he was always with God the Father, always living towards the Father, always in face-to-face communication and fellowship with the Father (John 1:1,2). So from the beginningless reaches of eternity the Father loved the Son, the Son loved the Father, and both loved and were loved by the Holy Spirit. Although God is one, he is also in a profound sense a family. Two of the divine persons of the Trinity are revealed to us by family names - the Father and the Son.

If this is true, then our love is not meaningless. One of the implications of our being made in the image of God is that we have the potential to love - to love God and to love our fellow human beings. The compassion of a father for his children, the gentle caress of lovers, the faithfulness unto death of the martyr - these are not random moves in some cosmic computer game, or the haphazard tricks of a blind fate. They are the meaningful and beautiful actions of noble beings in the presence of One who not only understands their feelings, but who is the origin of their love.

## Who defines love?

So far we have assumed that we know the meaning of the word *love*. This is a giant assumption in the modern world. 'I love you' can mean 'I want your body for the purpose of sexual satisfaction', which somehow does not have the same seductive sound! 'She left her husband and children for love' means 'She gave up the responsibilities of a legitimate relationship for the supposed freedom of an illegitimate one'. And on the lips of many contemporary theologians, the words 'God is love' means either that love (whatever that is) is god, or else that there is no such thing as sin.

How far removed such love is from Christian love! It is so different that it really requires another word to describe it. But of course it is one of the great tragedies of the twentieth century that beautiful, meaningful words have been emptied of their content and meaning, and used as mere connotation words. Love has become primarily a feeling, an emotion, a sensual or sentimental experience. At worst love has become a convenient connotation word for getting one's own way. One of the problems is that English has only one word for love, whereas the Greek of the New Testament age had four - *eros* (sexual love), *storgé* (family affection), *philia* (friendship) and *agapé* (charity). It was mainly *agapé* that the New Testament writers chose to describe the love God showed in Christ. For one reason or another the other words were unsuitable - *eros* was the love of the one who deserved to be loved, and *storgé* or *philia* was the love of those with whom we had natural ties of affection. The early Christians wanted a word that had the idea of undeserved love. *Agapé* was such a word. Into it the New Testament writers poured the full meaning of the active, self-giving, unmerited love of God in Christ. In this they were following the example of the Septuagint translation of the Old Testament into Greek, where *agapé* is used to translate the Hebrew word for love.

To indicate the radical effects of the work of Christ, *agapé* is used not only of God's love for us but also for our love for God and our love of our fellow Christians, our neighbours and our husbands and wives. Christ's love has defined the quality of Christian love. Therefore, we cannot use the word love with Christian overtones unless we mean the quality of love which Christ showed.

The One who is love has defined love. In the New Testament we find two passages which are virtual definitions of love - Romans 5:8 and 1 John 4:10:

'God demonstrates his own love for us in this: while we were still sinners, Christ died for us '(Romans 5:8); 'This is love: not that we loved God but that he loved

us and sent his Son as an atoning sacrifice for our sins'
(1 John 4:10).

From these and other verses we can construct a definition
of love in Christian terms. Love is the deliberate, kindly
pursuit of the highest good of another person, irrespective
of desert and cost.

First, it is clear that Christian love is not only an emotional thing. Love must act for the benefit of another. 'God
so loved the world that he gave . . . .' (John 3:16).
Nevertheless, the emotions are involved too, along with
the reason and the will. God's love for us is compared to a
father's compassion for his children (Psalm 103:13), a
mother's love for her child (Isaiah 49:15) and a man's love
for his wife (Hosea 2:14). So love is kind (1 Corinthians
13:4) as well as being deliberate and active.

Second, it is the highest good that true love pursues.
God is not content merely with the physical or psychological health of his people. It is the eternal salvation of their
whole beings which his plan of redemption has as its end.
But involved in the spiritual bliss of being with Christ for
ever is the resurrection of the body made fit for a renewed
universe, where tears shall be wiped away and there will
be no more pain.

Third, the divine love is irrespective of desert. It is not
those who deserve God's love who get it, but precisely
the reverse. It was while we were still sinners, enemies of
God, that he loved us. God, in Christ, loves the vile, the
corrupt, the vicious. He unites with his Son all who trust
in him, and because we are united to him we are pure
and spotless and righteous in his sight. But in ourselves
we do not deserve his love, only Christ deserves his love.

And fourth, God's love is irrespective of cost. God did
not withhold his only Son, but delivered him up for us all.
We are redeemed by the precious blood of Christ.
Because of the guilt of our sin and the justice of God, ours
is a costly salvation. It demanded a spotlessly righteous
substitute to provide a donated righteousness for sinners
and to endure the penalty of death due to them. Only
God's Son could satisfy the demands and God did not

withhold him. The Father willingly gave and the Son willingly came, out of love.

So we see that the Bible not only has the explanation of why there exists such a thing as love, but it also gives us the standard by which all love must be measured.

## *Love and Law*

There is another area where an understanding of the meaning of the work of Christ is extremely important. That is the relationship between love and law. The tendency of the modern world is to see them virtually as opposites. Law is rules and requirements. Love is freedom from all that. The classic modern expression of this is Situation Ethics. In it love is the only criterion by which every situation of moral choice is viewed. In the name of love all kinds of previously unethical behaviour may be justified - lying, stealing, adultery, promiscuous and homosexual behaviour, abortion and prostitution. Typically, love is never defined. It is kept so vague that it means what the individual wants. Thus it is virtually indistinguishable from an existentialist ethic which advocates the simple exercise of the individual will. On such a basis it is morally indifferent whether we hurt or harm. Leonard Cohen, the writer, poet and singer, expressed it perfectly in his song *Story of Isaac*:

*'When it all comes down to dust,*
*I will kill you if I must*
*I will help you if I can*
*When it all comes down to dust,*
*I will help you if I must*
*I will kill you if I can'.*[2]

One may, of course, reach such amoral conclusions with intellectual integrity. But what is wholly indefensible is to reach such conclusions and seek to give them the veneer of Christian respectability by using the word *love* as an undefined connotation word.

The fact is that there is no contradiction between love and law in true Christianity. Jesus said that he had not come to abolish the law but to fulfil it (Matthew 5:17). He also said that if we love him we should keep his commandments (John 14:15). And Paul said that love is the fulfilling of the law (Romans 13:10). In spite of this it is often mistakenly assumed that Jesus contradicted the moral law of the Old Testament both by word and behaviour. This is simply not true. In the Sermon on the Mount, what Jesus contradicted was wrong interpretations of, or additions, to the law. For instance, the law does contain the command to love your neighbour, but it does not contain the popular corollary 'hate your enemy' (See Matthew 5:43 and Leviticus 19:18). Similarly, in his revolutionary behaviour in healing on the Sabbath, it was not the Fourth Commandment he was breaking but merely human traditions. It was his constant concern to uphold the moral law while opposing unloving regulations such as the 'Corban' rule which broke the Fifth Commandment (see Mark 7:9-13).

## Law and the Cross

However, it is particularly in Christ's death for sinners that we see the harmony between law and love. It was because God loved the world that he gave his Son (John 3:16) and it was because Christ loved sinners that he died for them (Romans 5:8). Yet, although it was love that was the motivating force, it was not love that demanded the death of Christ. It was law. If there had been another way for God to have saved sinners, he would surely have chosen it in preference to the death of his Son. But God would not (indeed we can say, could not) work against his own law. C.S. Lewis expresses this beautifully in his children's book *The Lion, the Witch and the Wardrobe*. The evil White Witch has just claimed the life of the traitor Edmund in terms of the Deep Magic (the law) and his sister Susan suggests to the Great Lion Aslan that he might work against the Deep Magic.

'  "Work against the Emperor's Magic?" said Aslan, turning to her with something like a frown on his face. And

nobody ever made that suggestion to him again'.[3]
Instead of working against the Deep Magic, Aslan died in
the place of the traitor, thus satisfying the law and saving
Edmund. And in accordance with what Lewis calls 'the
Deeper Magic from before the Dawn of Time', death started working backwards and Aslan came to life again. (In
this presentation of what the death of Christ is like, Lewis
is much nearer to the Biblical position than he was in his
earlier *Mere Christianity*, where he presents the atonement
in terms of a vicarious repentance akin to that proposed
by MacLeod Campbell).

This is the biblical position. God's love does not
destroy his law. He does not even set it aside. He fulfils its
requirements. Man had rebelled against God. God's law
demanded that man should be punished and that man
should render perfect obedience to God before he could
be accepted. Sinful man could be punished, but he could
not render perfect obedience to God's law. However,
what sinful man could not do, God's love did. His Son
became incarnate. He took a true human nature.
Therefore he was able both to suffer and die and to perfectly obey God's law in our place.

If God does not work against or set aside his moral law
even in his love for sinners, should we expect that he will
set it aside as his standard for human behaviour? The
answer of both Old and New Testaments is a resounding
'No!' Jesus makes this abundantly plain in his answer to
the question, 'Which is the greatest commandment in the
Law?' (Matthew 22:36-40):

' "Love the Lord your God with all your heart and with
all your soul and with all your mind". This is the first
and greatest commandment. And the second is like it:
"Love your neighbour as yourself". All the Law and the
Prophets hang on these two commandments.'

The first thing we need to notice is that love is an integral
part of the Old Testament law. The command to love is a
command. And the second thing is that Jesus does not say
that love contradicts the rest of the law, but rather the rest
of the law depends on love as the first principle. The clear

implication of this is that all other commandments in the moral law are consistent applications or extensions of love. Therefore, if we ask how is love to be expressed in a particular situation, the answer is found in the law of God.

## Love and Marriage

It is particularly in the area of sexual relationships and marriage that all this comes into sharp focus. Many recognise the intimate connection between Christianity and marriage.

'Christianity brought marriage into the world: marriage as we know it. Christianity established the little autonomy of the family within the greater rule of the State. Christianity made marriage in some respects inviolate, not to be violated by the State. It is marriage, perhaps, which has given man the best of his freedom, given him his little kingdom of his own within the big Kingdom of the State, given him his foothold of independence on which to stand and resist an unjust State. Man and wife, a king and queen with one or two subjects and a few square yards of territory of their own: this really is marriage. It is a true freedom because it is a true fulfilment, for man, woman and children'.[4]

These words come from a very surprising source. They were written by D.H. Lawrence. That fact, I think, should establish beyond dispute the unique impact of Christianity upon the family, and the unique place of the family within Christianity.

But there are some who would not share Lawrence's sympathetic viewpoint. Indeed we live at a time when the family is increasingly under attack. People speak disparagingly of the nuclear family. We have the twin attacks of homosexualism and extreme feminism. We have had at least since the Sixties the influence of the permissive society with its so-called sexual liberation; concern over faithfulness and guilt about sexual misdemeanours have become 'hang-ups' to be got rid of.

And there is divorce. Instead of being the legitimate

resort of the few, whose spouses have been unfaithful, it has become the escape clause for the many when the going gets rough. One in three marriages end in divorce, and 16,000 more children each year are affected by marriage break-up - over 400 per day!

Many people are becoming aware of the magnitude of the crisis confronting us, but are unable because of their own philosophy to do anything about it. The producer of a new radio series for teenagers (encouraging them 'to think more about emotions than sexuality') said the programme was planned after discovering the 'horrifying abortion statistics among young women', but he went on to say that the series would not be 'preaching or moralising'!

Preaching and moralising is exactly what is needed. But so many cannot bring themselves to it because they have no absolute standard of right and wrong from which to speak. The Christian should have no such problem. But often we are afraid to speak lest we be thought 'holier than thou'. The time has come to speak, come what may.

CHAPTER 6
# THE POWER OF LOVE

How is love to be expressed in sexual relationships? Is it just a matter of everyone doing what he thinks is the loving thing, which is often just a cover for selfishness and lust? Or does God give specific instructions and principles for the right expression of love? When we turn to the Bible, we discover it is very much the latter.

## *God created sex*

In particular, the expression of love in sexual relationships is governed by the seventh commandment and related laws. But these principles are directly related to the pattern God established from the beginning. We already noticed that one aspect of God's creating us in his own image is that he created us male and female. Now that not only gives us the basis for human community and relationships in general, but it also lays down the pattern of expression of legitimate love. God's creation of male and female teaches the normality of marriage.

Of the solitary Adam, God said, 'It is not good for the man to be alone. I will make a helper suitable for him' (Genesis 2:18). I am sure that means in part that the solitary human being is not the perfect expression of the image of God which is unity in community. But surely it also means that this solitary state was not good for Adam. There was no legitimate way in which his sexual potential could be fulfilled.

It clearly follows that the sexual relationship is good. Sexual attraction was most emphatically not, as is often popularly imagined, the original sin or the result of that sin. God declared that it was not good for the man to be alone. He then created the woman and brought her to the man. It was only after the creation of man, male and female, that 'God saw all that he had made, and it was very good'. God created sex and declared it good.

The fundamental biblical text on marriage is Genesis 2:24, which is quoted in the New Testament by both Jesus and Paul (Matthew 19:5, Ephesians 5:31):

'For this reason a man will leave his father and mother and be united to his wife, and they will become one flesh'.

God created man in his own image. But it would appear that the full expression of that image was only reached with the creation of woman. In other words the image of God is not perfectly expressed in the solitary individual Adam but in the marriage relationship of Adam and Eve. Yes, the individual human being expresses God's image, but human beings in relationship express it better and a man and woman in the married relationship best of all. This is because, as we have already seen, God is not a monolithic one. He is three in one. He exists in the perfect and (to us) mysterious community of three persons. But is there not also something beautiful and mysterious about the oneness of a man and a woman in love? The Christian at least knows why that mysterious beauty exists. It is a reflection of heaven on earth. Excepting the incarnate Son of God and his love for his people, it is the nearest thing to the divine in the world.

It is little wonder that the first recorded human utterance is a love song, a poem (Genesis 2:23):

*This is now bone of my bone*
*and flesh of my flesh;*
*she shall be called woman*
*for she was taken out of man'.*

But is not this romantic fantasy? Surely many marriages have been nearer to hell on earth than heaven on earth. This is no doubt true, but that is because the greater something is the more potential it has for evil as well as for good. The higher and more noble a creature the more it can be corrupted to evil. A man can do more harm than a dog, a king more than commoner, an archangel most of all.

Nevertheless, it is 'for this reason' that a man shall 'leave, cleave and become one flesh'. Ever since the differentiation of the human race into male and female there has been a yearning in the heart of man for the re-union of what has been separated. This is the origin of sexual attraction. And it is God who has caused it. And he caused it in Eden before the Fall. It is his precious gift to mankind. Sin may corrupt sex, but it never created it. Just as Melkor in Tolkien's *The Silmarillion* could corrupt elves into orcs, but he could not create them.[1]

## *Leaving*

According to Genesis 2:24 (and Matthew 19:5 and Ephesians 5:31) there are three components to marriage - leaving, cleaving (AV) and becoming one flesh. Leaving father and mother is what may be termed the legal or social aspect of marriage. Marriage is not a private matter. It is a public affair. It involves two people leaving their families and establishing a new social unit, a new family. This is not a matter of interest to the two of them alone. This public aspect is always and everywhere an essential component of marriage. It is what distinguishes it from merely 'living together'. Fundamentally it is not 'the piece of paper' that matters. It is the social recognition. This was true in New Testament times when there was documented marriage (*gamos engraphos*) and undocumented marriage (*gamos agraphos*), marriage with or without the piece of paper, we might say. And there is no hint in the New Testament that undocumented marriages were not accepted by the apostles as valid. Interestingly, this distinction between what was called regular and irregular marriages was maintained in Scotland until 1940. And still to this day a couple who have been living together ('cohabitation with habit and repute') can apply for public recognition of their relationship to the Court of Session.

Of course the normal procedure is that there is some kind of public ceremony and celebration. This varies from culture to culture. In Britain there are two possibilities - civil marriage by a registrar and religious marriage by a minister (or other recognised person). Both are equally valid from a Christian point of view, but a Christian would normally wish a Christian ceremony as he recognises that marriage has a spiritual dimension.

So what is a valid marriage? Concepts of legal validity may change and have changed. But valid marriage in biblical terms is best summed up in the words of the nineteenth century English judge, Lord Penzance, as 'the voluntary union for life of one man and one woman'. Marriage is a union, an intimate partnership and a mutual bond, distinguished from all other human relationships. It is also a voluntary union. There must be free mutual consent. This is clearly implied in the Pauline comparison between the marriage relationship and the relationship between Christ and his Church. They willingly love each other. That is why the bride and bridegroom say 'I do'. Marriage is also a permanent relationship - for life. Jesus said, 'What God has joined together let man not separate'. We shall see later that there are biblical grounds for divorce. But legitimate divorce is not man separating what God has joined together, but God separating what God has joined together. And of course, marriage is also a monogamous relationship. God did not create two wives for Adam or two husbands for Eve.

## Cleaving

Important though the public aspect of marriage is, it is not the most important. If there is not the personal cleaving to one another of love, then the public leaving is an empty shell. This is that desire to be with each other and to share everything with each other, that longing to please one another and to help one another which all true lovers know. This love is the most powerful of human emotions.

'Love is as strong as death, its jealousy unyielding as the grave. It burns like blazing fire, like a mighty flame. Many waters cannot quench love; rivers cannot wash it away. If one were to give all of his wealth for love, it would be utterly scorned' (Song of Songs 8:6,7).

This is the love that has been celebrated in song down

through the ages, celebrated even by our own cynical and sensuous age - *Can't Buy Me Love, Love Minus Zero/No Limit, The Miracle of Love, The Power of Love.* For many it is the one reality to cling on to in a world of plastic and junk, although no one seems to understand it. In fact in a machine universe it is the only mysterious thing left. Something more than animal sex, something more than self-interest. For many it is the only glimpse they ever get of the world beyond this, of eternal reality, the only hint that their neat mechanistic, humanistic explanations may be false. Only the Bible explains this love. We are made in the image of the God who is love, the God who created us male and female in order that we would love in a God-like way.

But tragically in our sin and rebellion we worship and serve the creature rather than the Creator. We make a god out of love, or our lovers, and like all the gods they fail us, because they cannot bear the weight of our dependence and worship. They were never meant to. God created Eve as Adam's helper, not his goddess. The love of man for woman and of woman for man, wonderful and valid at its own level, was never intended to vie with God's love for humanity and humanity's love for God. However, there is a proper relationship between the two loves. It is an analogical, or typical, relationship. Human marital love, valid at its own level, is also a picture or reflection of divine love.

This is a theme that runs through the Bible, recurring several times in the prophets but reaching its zenith in Paul's teaching in Ephesians 5:22-33. There the Apostle, in his customary manner, weaves together practical counsel for married couples and profound theology concerning the relationship of Christ and his Church. Wives are to submit to their husbands as the Church submits to Christ; husbands are to love their wives as Christ loves the Church. The love between man and woman is a parallel to the love between Christ and his Church. It is impossible to conceive of marriage being accorded a higher honour, or being placed in a more noble context.

## *Love, Honour and Obey*

The role of the woman in marriage is akin to the role of the Church in its relationship with Christ. There is no doubt that this apostolic doctrine is one of the most controversial at the present time in the whole area we are considering. It is conceived of as being sexist, as representing woman as being inferior and subservient. This raises extremely important questions and we will look at some of these in Chapter 7.

However, it must be stressed here that it is not just a bare command to submit. God, through his apostle, tells us the type of submission he expects. It is not the fearful, servile grovelling of the slave for a tyrannous master, but the voluntary, loving respect of the Church for her Redeemer. That is a high calling, and all the more difficult because even the very best of husbands fall far short of the perfection of Jesus Christ. But there is an even more amazing submission used in the New Testament as an example for wives - the submission of the incarnate Son of God to God the Father. In discussing the headship of man over woman in the Church in 1 Corinthians 11, the Apostle Paul states that 'the head of every man is Christ, the head of the woman is man, and the head of Christ is God'. We have already seen how the inter-personal relationship of man and woman is a type of the supreme inter-personal relationship of the Triune God. Man, male and female, was created in God's image. And the eternal Son, though co-equal with the Father, willingly submitted himself to his Father's will in his rôle as Redeemer. Similarly, the woman, though co-equal with the man, willingly submits herself to the man in his rôle as her husband.

Why is it the submission of the wife that is emphasised, not her love for her husband? The answer is probably that the greatest problem area for women in marriage is not their love, or affection, or desire for their husbands, but their willingness to submit to their husbands. It would appear that the correct interpretation of Genesis 3:16

('your desire will be for your husband, and he will rule over you') is 'your desire shall be to control your husband but he should master you'. Not only does this interpretation do justice to the particular Hebrew word for 'desire' (used also of sin's desire for Cain in Genesis 4:7), but it also fits the context. Eve's role in the Fall had involved taking the lead. This sinful desire of woman to have authority over her husband has continued as one of woman's besetting sins ever since. The Christian woman is asked to submit willingly to the God-appointed headship of her husband.

What does this mean in practice? It means that the wife wishes to discuss all important matters with her husband, especially matters concerning their relationship and their family. It means that she seeks his advice and his guidance. It means, particularly, that when the problem has been aired, the discussion held and there is still a difference of opinion, she allows him to take the decision and, when the decision is taken, she makes it unanimous. None of this requires a wife to do what is wrong. Sometimes we must obey God rather than men. There may come a time to disobey husbands as well as rulers.

## As Christ Loved the Church

Similarly, the particular concern for men is not that they should exercise their headship or that they should be sexually attracted to their wives, but that they should love their wives. The danger is that they will use their headship or their sexual attraction in an unloving way. So they are commanded to love their wives. This seems strange to our modern ears. Surely a command to love is a contradiction! But, as we have seen, Christian love is not primarily a romantic feeling or emotion (although it by no means necessarily excludes that). Love is action. Love is self-giving. Love is kind. In fact we are not left to guess at the type of love required. Husbands are told to love their wives as Christ loved the Church and gave himself up for her.

What an astounding standard of love! The headship of the man is to be like the headship of Christ which is not proud, self-seeking and domineering but humble, self-giving and kind. How has Christ loved the Church? He has loved the Church in coming down from heaven, in humbly taking the form of a servant, in giving himself completely for her salvation and in nourishing and cherishing her as his own body. Such is the quality of love required of all Christians, but it is required in a special way of the Christian husband.

It is all too easy for husbands to get caught up in their work, their friends, their hobbies, their cars and even their houses and gardens and neglect their wives. When a couple fall in love, how the man delights to spend time with his girlfriend, to talk, to take her out, to give her presents! His aim should be to continue that concern, that kindliness, that romance.

## One Flesh

Marriage is more than a socially recognised relationship and more than a personal loving relationship. It is essentially a sexual relationship. 'The two will become one flesh' (Matthew 19:5). It has become a commonplace that Christianity is prudish. It is not Biblical Christianity that is open to such a charge, whatever other kind may be. The Bible is candid about the physical aspect of marriage, whether in matter-of-fact passages like Genesis 2, or in the gloriously sensual and romantic poetry of the Song of Solomon.

Man has held three views of his body, says C.S. Lewis (and therefore three views of sex):

'First there is that of those ascetic Pagans who called it the prison or tomb of the soul .... a source of nothing but temptation to bad men and humiliation to good ones. Then there are the Neo-Pagans .... the nudists and the Sufferers from Dark Gods, to whom the body is glorious. But thirdly we have the view which St. Francis expressed by calling his body "Brother Ass" . . .

Ass is exquisitely right because no one in his senses can either revere or hate a donkey. It is . . . . both pathetically and absurdly beautiful. So the body'.[2]

This mysterious combination of qualities in the donkey is the subject of a moving little poem by G.K. Chesterton.

*When fishes flew and forests walked*
*And figs grew upon thorn,*
*Some moment when the moon was blood*
*Then surely I was born;*
*With monstrous head and sickening cry*
*And ears like errant wings,*
*The devil's walking parody*
*Of all four-footed things.*
*The tattered outlaw of the earth,*
*Of ancient crooked will;*
*Starve, scourge, deride me: I am dumb,*
*I keep my secret still.*
*Fools! For I also had my hour;*
*One far fierce hour and sweet:*
*There was a shout about my ears,*
*And palms before my feet.*[3]

A similar combination of the sublime and the ridiculous is to be found, C.S. Lewis believes, in the act of physical intercourse. 'Lovers, unless their love is very short-lived, again and again feel an element not only of comedy, not only of play, but even of buffoonery, in the body's expression of Eros ..... There is indeed at certain moments a high poetry in the flesh itself; but also, by your leave, an irreducible element of obstinate and ludicrous un-poetry'.[4]

The point is that the Bible encourages us to accept our bodies and our sexual natures as good gifts from God capable of giving us moments of ecstasy as well as times of frustration, being vehicles of beauty as well as of temptation. The Christian will accept neither the extreme of D.H. Lawrence's deification of sex, nor the extreme of T.E. Lawrence's revulsion at the physical.

The Christian's unashamed acceptance of the sensual and sexual in marriage can be expressed no better than by the Song of Solomon. Of course I am aware that for many centuries in the Christian Church the book has been interpreted as an allegory of the love between Christ and his Church. I believe this is mistaken. The Song of Solomon does not present itself as an allegory. It is not interpreted in allegorical terms by other parts of Scripture. It should be taken at its face value as a poem of human sexual love, in the same way that the book of Esther should be taken at its face value as a historical account of God's preservation of the Jewish people. This is not to say that it cannot teach us about the higher love of Christ for his Church. E.J. Young comments 'Not only does it speak of the purity of human love, but by its very inclusion in the Canon it reminds us of a love that is purer than our own'. But this must not be pushed too far. It reminds us of such a love simply because the Bible teaches quite clearly that the love of man for woman is a reflection of God's love for his people.

However, the Song of Solomon is a celebration of the pure physical expression of love between a man and woman. It teaches us there is nothing dirty or obscene about sex in its proper context, which is within marriage. It is for our joy and comfort and for the physical expression of our unity in love. There is no human oneness closer than that of a couple who are truly one flesh, in harmony emotionally, spiritually and physically. The same acceptance of sex as a good gift of God is expressed, if somewhat more prosaicly, by the Apostle Paul. In 1 Timothy 4:3-5, after warning against false teachers, he says:

'They forbid people to marry and order them to abstain from certain foods, which God created to be received with thanksgiving by those who believe and know the truth. For everything God created is good, and nothing is to be rejected if it is received with thanksgiving, because it is consecrated by the word of God and prayer'.

Marriage, including sexual expression, is a good gift of God and to be received with thanksgiving. Even more explicitly Paul says in 1 Corinthians 7:4,5:

'The wife's body does not belong to her alone but also
to her husband. In the same way the husband's body
does not belong to him alone but also to his wife. Do
not deprive each other except by mutual consent and
for a time, so that you may devote yourselves to
prayer'.

The Bible, in spite of its frank acceptance of sex, does not
go into detail about sexual technique. It respects the pri-
vacy and intimacy of marriage. Equally it does not forbid
whatever sexual intimacy is mutually acceptable. There is
a tremendous freedom in the exclusive loving relationship
of marriage. There is no need for husbands and wives to
feel guilty about what they both enjoy. Christian psychologist John White advises couples 'Be gentle, be kind, and
your caresses will be more likely to arouse your partner
erotically. Moreover be sensitive to what pleases, and
what displeases, frightens or disgusts your partner'.[5]

It is interesting that the foundation text of marriage
(Genesis 2:24) says nothing about the procreation of children. This is important. Although it is obvious that procreation may be a consequence of sexual intercourse, it is
not essential to its nature. The purpose of sex is wholly
served if it expresses the true loving unity of a married
couple. That is not to say that the procreation of children
and their upbringing in a loving relationship are not
important. The Bible places tremendous importance on
them. It is of course part of God's perfect plan that children should be conceived in loving tenderness, but the
purpose of sex can be achieved even if children are not
conceived or even not intended to be conceived.

Finally, the place for sexual expression is firmly within
the mutual trust and security of a life-long marriage relationship. But such a relationship does not suddenly come
into being. It is the result of the gradual process of falling
in love, going together and engagement. Throughout that
process not only is there an increasing emotional unity,
but there is also a pressure to increasing physical intimacy. The Bible does not give us any specific guidelines. But
if we are in such a position we should ask ourselves if our

behaviour towards one another is tending to increase the pressure towards full sexual commitment before we have fully committed ourselves in marriage. If so, we are playing with fire. We are in danger of introducing guilt and fear into the one human relationship where they should certainly be excluded.

We are only beginning to learn about love, even the most experienced of us. We are like little children paddling on the shore of God's great ocean of love. We must never lose that humility and that sense of wonder and excitement which Jennifer Rush sang about in The Power of Love:

*'We're heading for something*
*Some place I've never been.*
*Sometimes I'm frightened but I'm ready to learn*
*About the power of love'.*[6]

CHAPTER 7
# LOVE MINUS

In this chapter we will look at two movements which have constituted a growing threat to the Christian view of sex and marriage in the second half of the twentieth century - homosexualism and feminism. I realise that these movements are not without the support of some Christians, even evangelical Christians, but I believe they are mistaken and their views can be shown to be inconsistent with biblical Christianity. I recognise also that those involved in these movements have attempted to achieve some things that are good - for instance, the ending of persecution of those with a homosexual orientation, and the recognition of the rights of women in our society. However, in spite of that, I believe that these movements are having, in general, a most destructive effect upon the Christian institution of marriage.

## *Same sex love*

Homosexuality is one of the distinctives of the second half of the twentieth century. Until the Sixties the homosexual act was a criminal offence, but in the great movement for personal liberty the law was changed to exclude private homosexual behaviour between adults from prosecution.

As a result, homosexuality came out into the open. And now not being content with being tolerated by society, homosexual activists campaign stridently for 'gay rights'. In London they have even gone beyond that. In 1987 Ealing Borough Council had plans to 'combat heterosexism' in schools, 'to promote positive attitudes to homosexuality' and to 'remove heterosexist practices and materials' from the classroom.

However, the appearance of the killer disease AIDS, which is rife amongst homosexuals, has caused many to think again. But even here there is an attempt to cover up just how responsible the homosexual community have been for spreading the AIDS virus. Over 90% of AIDS cases in the UK are homosexual men.

What has the Bible to say about homosexuality? God's creation of the original human couple teaches that, whereas heterosexuality is good, homosexuality is not. When God saw that it was not good for the man to be alone, it was a woman he created for him, not another man. By this act God declared his will for human sexuality. But this does not just mean that heterosexuality is the ideal and homosexuality is a kind of second best. In both Old Testament and New Testament homosexual acts are described as sins.

'Do not lie with a man as one lies with a woman; that is detestable' (Leviticus 18:22).

'They exchanged the truth of God for a lie and worshipped and served created things rather than the Creator - who is forever praised. Amen. Because of this God gave them over to shameful lusts. Even their women exchanged natural relations for unnatural ones. In the same way the men also abandoned natural relations with woman and were inflamed with lust for one another. Men committed indecent acts with other men, and received in themselves the due penalty of their perversion' (Romans 1:25-27).

'Neither the sexually immoral nor idolaters nor adulterers nor male prostitutes nor homosexual offenders nor thieves nor the greedy nor drunkards nor slanderers nor swindlers will inherit the kingdom of God' (1 Corinthians 6:9,10).

These passages clearly show that God declares homosexual acts to be sinful. But before we consider that further, we must notice an interesting emphasis the Apostle Paul makes in the Romans passage.

## Homosexuality is a judgement of God

Paul is not here teaching that one day God will punish the Roman world for its homosexuality. Homosexuality is itself part of the punishment. 'Therefore, God gave them over . . . .'(v.24) 'Because of this, God gave them over . . . .' What is the sin for which homosexuality is the punishment? It is the sin of idolatry, of materialism, of worshipping the created thing instead of the Creator.

It is important to take account of the context. Paul is showing mankind's desperate need for the gospel. It's not just that man is miserable. He is under the wrath of God, because he has rejected the revelation of God and foolishly turned to idolatry. And this wrath is not only a future thing. It is being revealed now (v.18).

But is wrath Christian? There are those who think that it is dishonouring to God to say that he is angry, as if he were subject to fits of rage like a human being. But that is to misunderstand the Bible. God's anger is not capricious, arbitrary and unpredictable like the anger of the gods of Canaan or of Rome. Nor does he lash out in rage. He is slow to anger. Nor has he given no warning. His will is revealed not only in the Scriptures, but also in the consciences of men (Romans 1:19, 2:15).

But having said all that does not remove the concept of wrath from the Bible. It is there in Old Testament and New, in the teaching of Jesus and his apostles. To remove it is to de-christianise Christianity. It is also to ask for a chaotic, unjust and meaningless universe, where the righteous will always suffer and the evil will go scot-free.

How is God's wrath being revealed now? It is being revealed in his giving over of nations to immorality. Yes, the immorality will be punished, but the immorality itself is also a punishment. A nation where immorality, including homosexuality, is rife, is already under the judgement of God. Take our own nation. For over a century now the Bible has been attacked, undermined and rejected. People have turned from the only living and true God to gods of their own imagination and to material things. Therefore, ultimately, after due opportunity for repentance, God has punished spiritual adultery with physical adultery and all its dire consequences for society. He has punished the unnaturalness of idolatry with the unnaturalness of homosexuality.

It must be emphasised that God's temporal judgements do not necessarily fall on individuals, but on groups and nations. Man is a communal creature and the actions of the individual affect the group and vice versa. This means that the homosexual tendency of an individual is not necessarily a sign that that person is under God's judgement. He may be a Christian struggling against temptation. But the very existence of his tendency is an indication that his group, his nation, his people are under the judgement of God. Conversely, this truth also applies to those of us who are not guilty of this particular sin. 'No man is an island complete of himself. Send not for whom the bell tolls. It tolls for thee' (Donne). That homosexuality is rife in our society is a sign that we are all under the wrath of God.

## Homosexual activity is sinful

There are two groups of people who disagree strongly with this - those who believe homosexuality is entirely natural, and those who believe that it is an unfortunate affliction or illness.

On the basis of Scripture and plain common sense the Christian cannot accept that homosexuality is natural. The Bible teaches and common sense confirms that a man and a woman are designed for each other sexually. They fit together! Men are manifestly not designed for sexual activity with other men, nor women with women. Many of the tragic results of male homosexual activity, in particular, such as faecal incontinence, are ample testimony to that. But it is not only physically that homosexuals do not 'fit together'. The high incidence of promiscuity among homosexuals, many times higher than among heterosexuals, surely indicates the extreme difficulty, the impossibility almost, of establishing a faithful, stable homosexual relationship, which indicates in turn that homosexuals do not 'fit together' emotionally or domestically.

The position that homosexuality is merely an unfortunate affliction or illness is more complicated. There are, no doubt, various causes of a homosexual orientation, and not all of them are the homosexual's fault. We are born into an already fallen imperfect world and we bring an already corrupted human nature with us. This means (to apply Jesus' words about eunuchs) some are born homosexuals, some are made homosexuals by men and some make themselves homosexuals. We must understand those with genetic or hormonal defects and those who, in childhood or adolescence, were terrified or disgusted by aggressive and overdominating members of the opposite sex, or were deliberately perverted by older people.

But when we have said all that, we have only explained some of the reasons for homosexual temptation. We have done no more than what we could do in the case of an adulterer, an embezzler or a drunkard. We have not proved that homosexual acts ought to be excluded from the Christian category of sin.

Homosexual behaviour is clearly defined as and shown to be sin in both Old and New Testaments. The passages quoted earlier demonstrate that. In addition homosexual acts clearly contradict the positive principle in the seventh Commandment and in Genesis 2, the principle that it is God's will that man's sexual nature should find expression only in the permanent one man, one woman relationship.

However, it must always be remembered that homosexual activity is only one sin among many. Yes, it is evidence of the judgement of God on a society, but so too are gossip, greed and rejection of parental authority (see Romans 1:29ff). And yes, homosexual acts are among the sins that, if persisted in, exclude from the kingdom of God, but equally so do promiscuous heterosexual acts, theft, drunkenness and slander (see 1 Corinthians 6:9,10).

Nevertheless, homosexuality is sin, and as sin it brings its own judgement, even in this life. 'Men committed indecent acts with other men, and received in themselves the due penalty for their perversion' (Romans 1.27). Sin brings misery. Whatever a man sows that he shall also reap. AIDS is only the latest and most horrific result of uninhibited homosexual behaviour. I recognise that homosexual activity is not the only route by which AIDS is spread. The misuse of drugs and the contamination of blood products have also played their part, while in Africa promiscuous heterosexual activity has been largely responsible, but it is a fact that in America and Europe promiscuous homosexual activity has been the major factor.

## Candidates for salvation

Homosexual activity is sin. There can be no doubt that this is the teaching of God's Word. But from the way many people talk, you would think that was all Christianity has to say to the homosexual. That is only the beginning, an important beginning, but only a beginning nonetheless. Because homosexual activity is a sin, homosexuals are candidates for salvation. That is what Paul's whole presentation in Romans 1 - 3 is all about. He is not writing about sin and judgement as if this was the complete Christian message. It is only preparatory for the revelation of God's love in the gospel:

'But now a righteousness from God, apart from law, has been made known, to which the Law and the Prophets testify. This righteousness from God comes through faith in Jesus Christ to all who believe. There is no difference, for all have sinned and fall short of the glory of God, and are justified freely by his grace through the redemption that came by Jesus Christ' (Romans 3:21-24).

The Bible's emphasis on sin is not to drive us away from God to destruction and despair, but to show us our desperate need of the redemption accomplished by Christ, and to call us to faith in him. After all, the Christian message is one of forgiveness, and only a person who has done wrong can be forgiven. We find the same emphasis in 1 Corinthians 6:9-11. After listing the lifestyles (including homosexual ones) which exclude one from the kingdom of God, Paul says to the Corinthian Christians:

> 'And that is what some of you were. But you were washed, you were sanctified, you were justified in the name of the Lord Jesus Christ and by the Spirit of our God'.

Corinth was a notorious centre of all kinds of vice in the ancient world, and some of the Christians had been converted out of such a vicious background. There were even Christians who had been male prostitutes and homosexual offenders, but they had been transformed by the grace of God. They were freed from the vices that had once enslaved them. We are not told if they were all able to establish normal heterosexual relationships. No doubt some of them were. But possibly others were called to a celibate life, which Paul mentions in the next chapter of 1 Corinthians as a specific option for some Christians. At any rate, they were all given the grace and strength to live a new lifestyle.

The Gospel is a message of hope and the Church is a community of hope. The Church of Jesus Christ is made up 100% of moral failures. But they are moral failures who have been given a new life and a new lifestyle.

## Singleness

In this context it is important to recognise that, in addition to marriage, the New Testament teaches the legitimate option of the single life (and of course not only for those who suffer from a homosexual orientation). In response to the disciples' comment that it was better not to marry, Jesus said (Matthew 19:11-12):

> 'Not everyone can accept this word, but only those to whom it has been given. For some are eunuchs because they were born that way; others were made that way by men; and others have made themselves eunuchs because of the kingdom of heaven. The one who can accept this should accept it'.

In other words there are some for whom singleness is the norm, either because of physical abnormality, or because of ill treatment by others, or because of a specific Christian calling.

The teaching of the Apostle Paul in 1 Corinthians 7:7-9 is entirely in agreement with this:

'I wish that all men were as I am. But each man has his own gift from God; one has this gift, another has that. Now to the unmarried and the widows I say: It is good for them to stay unmarried, as I am. But if they cannot control themselves, they should marry, for it is better to marry than to burn with passion'.

Both our Lord and Paul are agreed that singleness is a legitimate option, but both also make it clear that it is a legitimate option only for those who are sexually abstinent. Jesus speaks of eunuchs rather than 'singles', and Paul speaks of the gift of control.

When all that has been said, however, it remains a fact that the Bible teaches the normality of marriage. 'It is not good for the man to be alone'. Only when God had created mankind male and female in a married state did he declare his creation to be very good (Genesis 1:27,31). Due to the fact that we live in a fallen, abnormal, imperfect universe, there are some for whom singleness is right, but the norm is marriage.

### Feminism

We must recognise that there have been sufficient grounds for the rise of the feminist movement in our society. For a long time women did not have equal rights with men. They were excluded from higher education, denied the vote, and unjustly discriminated against in employment. The gains made in these areas should be welcomed by all Christians. However, in its attack on the biblical view of marriage, modern feminism is a destructive force. In its over-enthusiastic throwing out of the bath water it is throwing out the baby, bath and all. There are two biblical doctrines in particular which feminists attack - the creation of woman and the headship of the husband.

It was not good for the man to be alone, so God created woman. But it is the method of creation which is so significant. God did not create woman totally separately from man. He created woman out of man.

'But for Adam no suitable helper was found. So the LORD God caused the man to fall into a deep sleep; and while he was sleeping he took one of the man's ribs and closed up the place with flesh. Then the LORD God made a woman from the rib he had taken out of the man, and he brought her to the man' (Genesis 2:20b-22).

This is part of the creation account which is so ridiculed today particularly by feminists. The magazine 'Spare Rib' was sarcastically named after it. The account is understood to be demeaning to women. However, feminists thus miss the whole point. What hypothetical alternative would they prefer? That God created man and woman from different sources? Then indeed there could be a basis for inequality! Or do they prefer a complete alternative to the Christian philosophy? The contemporary forms of impersonalism are not encouraging, haunted as they are by the spectres of Nietzsche, Nazism and the Marquis de Sade. The problem, succinctly put, is that if there is no God 'outside' the universe, and therefore no values independent of the universe, then what exists is right, or might is right. On such a basis the conclusion of de Sade is difficult to avoid. Man is physically more powerful than woman, therefore he can use woman for his pleasure.

The fact is that only the Christian faith in general, and the Genesis account of the origins of the human race in particular, give a firm foundation for the equality of men and women. We all derive our humanity from the one source, from Adam. We are one human race differentiated into male and female. (It is interesting to note that the essential oneness of the human race in Adam prohibits not only sexism, but also racism, as Paul emphasises in Acts 17:26). It is probably not without significance also that Eve was formed out of Adam's rib. 'Not made out of his head to rule over him, nor out of his feet to be trampled upon by him, but out of his side to be equal with him, under his arm to be protected and near his heart to be beloved', as Augustine put it.

## *Headship and submission*

As we already saw in the previous chapter, the Bible teaches the headship of the husband in marriage and the submission of the wife to her husband. The classic passage is Ephesians 5:22-24:

'Wives, submit to your husbands as to the Lord. For the husband is head of the wife as Christ is head of the Church, his body, of which he is the Saviour. Now as the church submits to Christ, so also wives should submit to their husbands in everything'.

There is no doubt that this apostolic doctrine is one of the most controversial at the present time in the whole area we are considering. It is conceived of as being sexist, as representing woman as being inferior and subservient.

Sexual inequality and the maltreatment of women are extremely important questions and no Christian should treat them lightly. However, because of the pressure of feminism, many feel forced either to modify their understanding of the Bible or to reject it altogether. The most common attempt to modify is by explaining such parts of the Bible as culturally conditioned or merely the product of the personality of Paul. But if that is so, then who is to decide which parts of the Bible are authoritative and which are not? Why should Paul's teaching about the relationship of Christ and the Church be any less culturally conditioned than his teaching about marriage? And how do we account for Christ's viewing himself as the Bridegroom and the Church as the Bride in the Gospels and in Revelation? We find that not only apostolic authority but dominical authority too has slipped through our fingers.

If we reject the authority of Christ and his apostles, we are rejecting Christianity, and if we reject Christianity, we are rejecting the one movement in the world that down through history has worked for the true liberation of women. Simply compare the position of women in those countries which have been most influenced by the Christian gospel with their position in Hindu or Moslem cultures. The simple fact is that Northern European culture has given a dignity and equality to women unparalleled in the world. And it has done so simply because of the pervasive effect of the Bible and the teaching and attitude of Jesus in particular. Jesus safeguarded the rights of women in a remarkable way in his teaching on marriage and divorce (Matthew.19:8,9) and in his public ministry he showed just as much concern for women as for men, totally disregarding conventions of the time. He spoke with women in public , he helped women in distress, he accepted women as his followers. This attitude is summed up supremely by the Apostle Paul when he asserts that there is neither male nor female but we are all one in Christ Jesus (Galatians 3:28). Men and women stand equal in being created in the image of God. They stand equal in their sin and rebellion against God. And they stand equal in salvation when they trust in Jesus Christ.

Nevertheless, the same Bible which makes that glorious assertion also requires wives to submit to their husbands. How are we to reconcile these two apostolic teachings? The contradiction between them is only apparent. In a democracy like ours is there any contradiction between believing on the one hand that all are equal before the law, and on the other that some have positions of leadership and authority over others? Of course not. The headmaster and the teacher, the captain and the sergeant, the manager and the worker are all equal, but some are to lead and some are to submit to leadership. Similarly in the marriage relationship the man is called to be the head and the woman is called to submit to his leadership. Submitting to authority does not imply inferiority. Nor are women asked to be submissive to all men - only to their own husbands.

CHAPTER 8
# THROWAWAY RELATIONSHIPS

Given the central importance of love in Christianity, is love all you need? Specifically, is love all you need in human relationships? Ever since that day in 1967 when the Beatles sang 'All You Need is Love' to a worldwide television audience of 150 million people, it has been taken for granted that love is indeed all you need. As long as two people love each other that's all that counts. It doesn't matter if they aren't married. It doesn't matter if they are already married. It doesn't matter if they are of the same sex. It doesn't matter if tomorrow they're going to love others. All that matters is that today they love each other.

'It is ridiculous to think you can spend your entire life with just one person. Three is about the right number. Yes, I imagine three husbands would do it'. So says Clare Booth Luce.[1] The anthropologist Margaret Mead suggests that we accept the concept of 'serial monogamy' - being faithful to one partner at a time. Others, as a result of the so called 'sexual revolution' of the Sixties and Seventies, see nothing wrong with promiscuous sexual relationships. If you are attracted to someone, why not have sex with them? Sexual intercourse is natural. Why should we have hang-ups about it? Even although the threat of AIDS demands a radical rethink of these attidudes, there seems little evidence that it is taking place.

We saw in Chapter 6 that when God made Adam, he said that it was not good for man to be alone. We saw in Chapter 7 that when he made another human being to be a suitable helper for Adam, he did not make another man, he made a woman. But it is also true that he made one woman, not many. God's pattern of sexual relationship for the human race is a permanent, one man-one woman relationship and he declares every aberration from that to be sinful, whether it be fornication or adultery, pre-marital or extra-marital sexual activity, or unjustified divorce. There exists the idea that heterosexual promiscuity is somehow less sinful, more natural, more normal than homosexuality or other sexual deviations. But if God's will for human sexual relationships is revealed (as I believe it is) in the creation of the original human couple, then any deviation from that is sinful, unnatural and abnormal. This is confirmed by the seriousness with which fornication and adultery in particular are consistently viewed in the Bible.

In the rest of this chapter I wish to consider the main heterosexual sins - premarital and extramarital sex and unjustified divorce. But first we must consider an attack that is often made on Christian sexual ethics.

## *The Two*

One of the first objections which people make to 'biblical morality' is that polygamy is not prohibited in the Bible. This is certainly true of the Old Testament. But although it was not prohibited in the Mosaic law, it formed no part of God's original pattern for human sexuality, which as we have seen, was that 'a man shall leave his father and mother, cleave to his wife (not wives) and they shall be one flesh' (Genesis 2:24). But the Old Testament does more than that. It describes for us in some detail what happens when that pattern is ignored. The histories of Abraham's, Jacob's, David's and Solomon's polygamy and the subsequent divisive effects on their families are faithfully described, leaving us in no doubt as to the rightness of God's original pattern. The tragic rivalries between Isaac and Ishmael, between Joseph and his brothers, between Absalom and Amnon and between Adonijah and Solomon were all exacerbated, if not directly caused by, the polygamy of their fathers. And the extreme polygamy of Solomon had disastrous consequences in the division of his empire into the northern kingdom of Israel and the southern kingdom of Judah during the reign of his son.

The reason for the failure of polygamy is not difficult to find. The intimacy and exclusive loyalty required by God's image-bearer in his sexual relationships as a basis for family life is seriously compromised, if not destroyed, by polygamous relationships. There is a possessiveness, a jealousy proper to true love which is frustrated by polygamy and turned into envy and contempt (as in the cases of Sarah and Hagar, and Hannah and Peninnah).

However clear the Old Testament picture is, the New Testament one is even clearer. In answer to a question about divorce, Jesus gave emphatic support to monogamy as the only rightful form of marriage, quoting Genesis 2:24 in such a way as to make it obvious that it concerns an exclusive relationship - '*the two* will become one flesh' (Matthew 19:5).

## *Adultery New and Old*

What exactly does the Bible teach about sex outside marriage? Many people who would regard themselves as Christians think that there is nothing wrong with sex outside marriage as long as it is done in the name of 'love'. But what does God say in his Word? He says, 'You shall not commit adultery'. 'Oh, but that's Old Testament!' is the modern response. That argument is simply irrelevant unless it can be shown that Jesus or his apostles declared that that part of the Old Testament is not now applicable in the Christian age. I challenge anyone to find any New Testament teaching which declares that adultery is no longer sin.

On the contrary, Jesus says to the woman taken in adultery, 'Go and sin no more' (John 8:11). And far from alleviating the force of the seventh commandment, he intensifies it by saying (in the Sermon on the Mount, supposedly so revered by modern Christians), 'But I tell you that anyone who looks at a woman lustfully has already committed adultery with her in his heart'. Neither does the rest of the New Testament provide a haven for those John White calls 'the New Adulterers'. The Apostle Paul lists fornicators and adulterers among those excluded from the kingdom of God (1 Corinthians 6:9,10) and he lists sexual immorality and impurity among the works of the flesh

(Galatians 5:19-21).

In addition to giving us the Maker's instructions for the right way for us to live, the Bible also gives us case histories of those who ignored these instructions. The classic case of adultery in the Bible is that of King David with Bathsheba (2 Samuel 11 and 12). This has several important things to teach us.

It reminds us that anyone can commit adultery. David was one of the greatest saints of God in Old Testament times. He is the man after God's own heart. He is the sweet psalmist of Israel. He is the king with the shepherd's heart. Yet he committed adultery, and that in a most aggravated fashion. There is no one who is exempt from the temptation to commit adultery. Let him that thinks he stands take heed lest he fall.

It warns us about the road to adultery. David did not set out with the deliberate intention of committing adultery. He slid into it. He was lazing about in Jerusalem when he should have been commanding his army. He got up from his bed in the evening (!) and he just happened to see a beautiful woman bathing. Well, he couldn't help that. He could have turned away and put it out of his mind. But he didn't. He found out who she was - 'Bathsheba, the daughter of Eliam and the wife of Uriah the Hittite'. And then he sent messengers to get her. She came and he slept with her. One step led to another. It seemed inevitable. But it need not have been. At any point in the process he could have stopped short of adultery. He didn't. He was being driven on by his sexual desire for this beautiful woman and that took precedence over everything else - over his responsibility to his family, over the trust Uriah had in him, over his status as king, over his status as a believer. Maybe he made excuses for himself. Maybe he thought polygamy was an excuse. Maybe he thought he could do as he wanted because he was king. Maybe he thought no one would ever know. Or maybe he just didn't think.

David's case also teaches about the destructive consequences of adultery. Bathsheba was pregnant. It happens.

Even with modern contraception it happens. At least David didn't try to procure an abortion, but death resulted none the less. David tried to cover up. He sent for Bathsheba's husband Uriah and tried everything he knew to get him sleep with his wife, so that he would think the child was his, all to no avail. David could not face the public shame that would result. He did the unthinkable. He sent a letter by Uriah's own hand to his General Joab to have Uriah killed. What a betrayal! And that is what adultery is - betrayal. John White comments:

> 'It is not copulation that is the 'wicked' thing in betrayal. Copulation is good (just as apples are good). It is stealing and cheating that make adultery bad, not copulation'.[2]

But that betrayal was only the beginning of the dire consequences of David's adultery. Alexander Whyte pictures Joab giving David a long hard stare and silently tapping his breast pocket (where the letter was kept) whenever there was any tension between them. But even worse was the contempt which David's behaviour caused God's enemies to show, even in his own family. It is no accident that the Bible proceeds immediately to describe David's son Amnon's rape of his half-sister Tamar, and the subsequent hatred of Absalom for Amnon which sowed the seeds of discord that were finally to tear the country apart in civil war. David had lost his moral authority.

The same is still true today. Adultery is supposed to be all right. We should be mature enough to handle it. But who trusts the politician who betrays his wife? What child still trusts the father who has been unfaithful to his mother? We hear a great deal today about the loss of respect for authority. How much of it is due to the fact that fathers and politicians and ministers of religion and others in positions of authority have lost their own moral authority?

Is that it? Is that all the Bible has to say about David's adultery? Just a word of condemnation? A thousand times no! God sent the prophet Nathan to him not just to condemn his sin but to touch his heart and cause him to come to repentance. Nathan's famous 'Thou art the man'

produced David's 'I have sinned against the LORD'. He
was then assured that the LORD had taken away his sin.
We miss the whole point not only of this incident but of
the whole of the Bible, if we think the message stops with
condemnation and guilt. Jesus condemned the adulterous
woman's sin (he called it sin), but he did not condemn
her. He came into the world not to condemn the world,
but that the world through him might be saved. But none
can be saved until they realise their guilt, until they realise
they need to be saved.

## Marriage After Sex?

The biblical standard is quite clear. The life-long faithful
commitment of marriage is the proper context for the intimacy of sexual intercourse. Sex outside or before marriage is wrong. This is part of God's law - the law that
reflects the faithfulness and love of God - the law that is
the only way to our lasting fulfilment, because it is the
Maker's instruction, because it is his way, and because we
are made in his image.

Of course fallen man has never accepted this. Because
sexual pleasure is the most intense physical pleasure
known to human beings, we have wrested it from its
proper place. We desire it for itself. We worship it as a
goddess. The Canaanites called her Ashtaroth, the Greeks
Aphrodite and the Romans Venus. Today we are cleverer.
We have captured the greatest word in the English language with all its Christian overtones, and we call her
Love. Norman Mailer in describing the attitude of the
post-war Beat generation says it explicitly. Love is not the
search for a mate, but 'the search for an orgasm more
apocalyptic than the one which preceded it'. God 'is locat-
ed in the senses of the body; not the God of the churches
but the unachievable whisper of mystery within the sex,
the paradise of limitless energy and perception just
beyond the next wave of the next orgasm'.[3]

And so the girl really believes the boy who says he
wants to love her, or give her all of his love, or any one of

a thousand pop song clichés. She thinks he really does love her. He's maybe meaning something else entirely. Of course in the past this was connected with the notorious 'double standard' of men, who expected to sow their wild oats and then have virgin brides. But now, due in large measure to the Pill and freely available abortion, women can sow their wild oats too. And tragically, the effect of feminism on this has not been to make men more caring, but to make women less caring; not to bring men up to the feminine conception of love, but to bring women down to the masculine level. Now it is commonplace for women to be just as physical and promiscuous in their attitude to sexual relationships as men tended to be.

What have we got to show for all this worship of Venus, all this throwing off of the restrictions of 'rigid morality'? Where are all the fulfilled and balanced people we were promised? Where are the liberated ones? Where is the new society? Instead we have filled the world with lonely, neurotic, guilt-ridden and frustrated people, we have opened up a pit of miserable slavery to perversion for many, and we have given society the bill for the countless abortions, the epidemic of sexually transmitted diseases and the spectre of AIDS. Dylan's 'Chimes of Freedom' are still

> *'Tolling for the aching ones whose wounds*
> *cannot be nursed*
> *For the countless confused, accused, misused,*
> *strung-out ones and worse*
> *An' for every hung-up person in the whole*
> *wide universe*
> *An' we gazed upon the chimes of freedom flashing'.*[4]

## *Marriage After Marriage*

The most common effect of this sexual 'liberation' is the break-up of marriages. But there is another important factor in marriage break-up, as Os Guinness (playing the devil's advocate) points out in *The Gravedigger File* -

'Most modern people have a relationship to their

choices that's closer to the model of the Kleenex tissue than to that of the silk handkerchief . . . .

What may be trifling at the level of things becomes telling at the level of relationships, societies, and - above all - faiths. What happens when modern people 'run through' homes like disposable handkerchiefs? Better still, when they 'run through' marriages? Above all, when they 'run through' beliefs?

. . . . once change has been considered appropriate and necessary, and marriage has been boiled down to one thing (the make-or-break achievement of emotional intimacy), faithfulness can easily be made to look constricting and hopelessly old fashioned, "the sure recipe for a loveless marriage"'.[5]

Although there may be discussion about the underlying causes, there is no doubt about the facts. At the beginning of the century in Scotland there were less than 200 divorces. In 1985 there were 13,370. Approximately one marriage in four ends in divorce (one in three in England). In the USA the situation is even worse, where even some conservative Christians advocate divorce where the partners feel themselves to be incompatible not only emotionally but also in their views of Christian doctrine! 'Disobeying Christ out of faithfulness to Christ!' comments Os Guinness, 'The irony is exquisite'.[6]

What does Christ say in his Word about divorce? In answer to a question from the Pharisees (some of whom held a very lax view of divorce) Jesus emphasised first of all the permanency of marriage. 'What God has joined together, let man not separate' (Matthew 19.6). But then (in v.9) he allows one exception -

'I tell you that anyone who divorces his wife, except for marital unfaithfulness (fornication), and marries another woman commits adultery'.

In other words he says quite clearly that the person who divorces his/her spouse for marital unfaithfulness is free to marry again. This understanding of the passage has been disputed, but after careful exegesis John Murray concludes that it is correct:

'In simple terms it means that divorce in such a case dissolves the marriage and that the parties are no longer man and wife'.[7]

There is only one other ground for divorce recognised by the New Testament. That is desertion. In 1 Corinthians 7:10-16 the Apostle Paul supplements the teaching of Jesus about divorce. (When in this context Paul says 'not I, but the Lord' and 'I, not the Lord', he is not making some distinction between his inspired and uninspired writings. He is distinguishing between what Jesus said in his earthly ministry - in Matthew 19, for example - and what he himself is now adding with the authority of an apostle of Christ, about a new situation). After making clear that a Christian must not divorce a spouse simply because he/she is a non-Christian, he adds 'But if the unbeliever leaves, let him do so. A believing man or woman is not bound in such circumstances; God has called us to live in peace'.

While I agree with John Murray that this verse is allowing divorce with the right of re-marriage, I cannot accept his conclusion that this 'Pauline privilege' only applies to Christians whose non-Christian spouses have deserted them.[8] The difference of opinion concerns the *application* of the 'Pauline Privilege' to real life situations, not the exegesis of the passage. It is quite clear that Paul is talking about a Christian being deserted by a non-Christian. There is no disagreement on that score. The disagreement comes at the point of applying the principle. John Murray says it applies only to the specific case mentioned by Paul (desertion of a Christian by a non-Christian), whereas I agree with the framers of the Westminister Confession that the principle applies to any case of wilful and irremedial desertion.[9] What convinces me that this is indeed correct is that Paul does not specify that the reason for the desertion is religious incompatibility. He talks of simple desertion. It could be for any reason - not necessarily for the reason that the unbeliever can't stand the believer's Christianity. And when we come to construct a legal system on Christian principles, it is surely contrary to natural justice to allow a privilege to Christians which is denied to non-Christians. If a Christian is allowed a divorce on the simple grounds of desertion, then a non-Christian must be also.

Where, then, does the biblical position on divorce differ from the contemporary legal one? First, the Bible makes a fundamental distinction between a guilty and an innocent party. This does not imply that one party is wholly wrong and the other wholly right. It means that one party is guilty of adultery or desertion and the other is not. And only the innocent party can seek a divorce. This was also the legal position in Scotland until well into this century. With the passing of the Divorce (Scotland) Act in 1976 there are no guilty or innocent parties.

Second, the only basis for divorce now is 'the irretrievable breakdown' of the marriage, for which various grounds - adultery, desertion, 'unreasonable' behaviour and non-cohabitation - can be cited as evidence. As we have seen, the Word of God gives only two grounds for divorce - adultery and desertion. The present position is virtually divorce on demand. Of the 13,370 divorces granted in 1985 the vast majority (11,455) were granted for 'unreasonable' behaviour or non-cohabitation (for 2 years with consent or 5 years without consent).[10]

There is no doubt that the contemporary situation is giving great headaches to Churches and ministers as couples approach them for re-marriage after divorce. But these are nothing compared to the heartaches which people are giving themselves in broken homes and broken families. The Churches will be able to cope with the problems even as the New Testament Church dealt with the appalling irregularity of marital status in centres of vice like Corinth. But how are divorcees coping with the legacy of guilt and bitterness? Second marriages break down at a faster and higher rate than first. A recent study has found that a majority of divorced people felt that they should have been reconciled to their first partners. And how are the children coping? The ones who have two fathers or two mothers, one of whom they call their 'real' father or 'real' mother. The ones who compare the presents their 'real' father or mother gives them with those which step-father or step-mother gives. The ones who say 'I don't have to do what you tell me. You're not my real father anyway'.

How are any of them ever going to cope unless they come to know the healing power of Jesus Christ? The Christ who sat at a well talking to a woman who had been divorced five times and was now living with another man. The Christ who exposed her innermost longings, her guilt and her questions, of whom she said 'Come, see a man who told me everything I ever did. Could this be the Christ?' (John 4:29). The Christ who, through his apostle, reached out to the broken ones, the degraded ones, the guilty ones, the defiled ones in Corinth and assured them that they were washed, sanctified and justified in his name.

# PART 3

# LIBERTY

CHAPTER 9
# CHRISTIAN LIBERATION

The longing for liberty, whether personal or political, is a great human aspiration. Nor is it a recent aspiration. The framers of the Scottish Declaration of Arbroath said they were fighting for freedom 'which no true man will surrender but with his life' - a sentiment immortalised by Robert Burns in 'Scots wha hae':

*By Oppression's woes of pains*
*By your sons in servile chains*
*We will drain our dearest veins*
*But they shall be free.*[1]

This longing for freedom from oppression was given a great impetus and direction by the Reformers and Covenanters in Scotland who laid the basis of our modern freedoms with their opposition to the tyranny of men's consciences by Rome and by the Stuart kings. However, such legitimate longing for freedom from oppression was superseded in the eighteenth century Enlightenment by a desire for freedom from all restraints. This desire was expressed most forcefully by Jean-Jacques Rousseau - 'Man was born free, but everywhere he is in chains!' His concept of freedom has had a marked effect on education. He argued that the best education was virtually an absence of education. Karl Marx, in the nineteenth century, carried this emphasis on freedom to its logical conclusion in the area of economic and political theory - 'Workers of the world unite. You have nothing to lose but your chains!' Today we hear much of liberation - gay liberation, women's liberation, liberation theology. The irony is that man is still in chains, and more in chains than ever where these ideas are influential. Many can identify with the words of Leonard Cohen:

*Like a bird on a wire*
*Like a drunk in a midnight choir*
*I have tried in my way to be free.*[2]

Man's attempts at freedom have proved futile, but still he

longs for freedom. Why is this? Could it be that he fails to recognise the real tyranny from which he must be freed? And the real Liberator? Hear what Jesus has to say: 'I tell you the truth, everyone who sins is a slave to sin . . . . if the Son sets you free, you will be free indeed' (John 8:34,36). Jesus says that the essential tyranny is that of sin, and the essential freedom is freedom from sin. This is the very root of the Christian view of liberty.

In Romans 3:23-25 (AV) the Apostle Paul uses three words to describe this liberation in Christ - justified, redemption, propitiation:

'For all have sinned and come short of the glory of God; being justified freely by his grace through the redemption that is in Christ Jesus: whom God hath set forth to be a propitiation . . . .'

To help you to understand these three words, justification, redemption and propitiation, I want you to use your imagination. I want you to stand in three places. I want you to stand in a courtroom, in a concentration camp and at an altar on a mountain top.

## Not guilty

The scene is a court of law. There are all the familiar items - the judge's bench, the witness stand, the jury box and the dock. But as you look round you realise that this is no ordinary courtroom. The judgement seat is the throne of the universe and God himself sits upon it. It is not with the laws of the land that this court deals but with the laws of the universe. To your horror you realise that you stand in the dock. You stand accused of breaking these laws. You are on trial for your life - your eternal life.

God calls for the testimony of witnesses. The first witness is tall and fair and clad in the greys and greens of mountain and forest. She is Nature. 'Did you reveal me to the accused?' God asks. 'O yes,' she replies and her voice is like the music of the sea, 'I showed him your creative power and divine glory'. Then a horrible wrinkled thing crawls into the witness box. It is painted like an aged whore. It is Sin. And you marvel that it once appeared to you as a beautiful woman. 'Do you know the accused?' God asks. 'Ah yes,' it croaks with a grotesque smile, 'we know each other well. Many are the happy hours we spent in each other's company'. You wish the ground would swallow you up.

Your mind reels as God calls for the verdict from the jury. In dismay you hear your own conscience say 'Guilty!' the law of your society say 'Guilty!' and the law of God say 'Guilty!' The sentence is pronounced, 'The wages of sin is death', and the officers are about to lay strong hands upon you to lead you away, when a great voice calls from the centre of the throne, 'Lay no hand on him, he is mine'. And behold, down from the throne there steps the High King over all kings bearing in his body the scars of an ancient victory, and he says, 'I was wounded for his transgressions, I was bruised for his iniquities, and the punishment that brings him peace was upon me. Therefore I declare him not guilty'.

That is the meaning of justification.  Christ died, the just in the place of the unjust, so that the guilty might have their guilt removed. This justification is received by trusting Christ alone.

## Freedom at a Price

The second place you must stand is in a concentration camp. All the misery and torment of the concentration camp are there - the brutal guards, the unrelenting labour, the gas chamber. But the guards have strange names. One is called Pride, another Greed, another Lust and yet another Cruelty. They all promise you happiness and relief if you will obey them. If you steal from your fellow prisoners, betray your friends and tell lies about the smoke from the chimney, you will be rewarded with choice morsels. But for every moment of pleasure there are days of tedious misery and frustration, and soon the choice morsels become dry husks. You come to hate yourself for your weakness and the guards for their deception.

At that moment the walls shake and the cry goes up, 'Liberated! We're free! The Liberator has come!' The guards flee from the wrath of his face and he gently leads you out. You are free!

That conveys something of the meaning of redemption. It is liberation from slavery, it is a setting free. But again it has to be remembered that the freedom is bought at a great cost. No liberation is cheap. The liberation of Nazi-occupied Europe cost hundreds of thousands of lives. The liberation of sinners cost the life of the Son of God. Redemption is freedom purchased at a price.

## *Wrath Removed*

The third place I want you to stand is by an altar on a mountain top. This scene is less familiar to our modern eyes than the courtroom and the concentration camp. To help you to understand it you should read Leviticus 1 and 16 and Genesis 22.

You have just climbed the mountain with your father to worship God by building an altar and offering a sacrifice. On the way up you suddenly realised that you had the wood and the fire and the knife, but no lamb. You were puzzled because you knew that the anger of God at sin could only be turned away by the sacrifice of a lamb. How often you had seen your father sadly and solemnly lay the lamb on the altar, cut its throat and burn the carcass. 'Where is the lamb for the burnt offering?' you asked your father. 'God himself will provide the lamb for the burnt offering, my son', he replied.

Now you watch your father as he gathers the stones, builds the altar and lays the wood on it. Then to your horror he takes hold of you and lays you on the altar. In disbelief you see him take the knife, tears in his eyes. 'Is there really no way for God's anger to be turned away from my sins then?' you wonder. 'Will God not provide a lamb to atone for my sins, to appease God?' Then wonder of wonders, a voice speaks to your father from heaven, 'Do not lay a hand on the boy!' Your father looks up and catches sight of a sheep caught by its horns. In a few minutes you are standing by your father's side, your trembling hand in his, watching through new eyes the sacrifice of the lamb who dies in your place.

That is what propitiation is - the appeasement of an offended God by the death of the God-appointed substitute in the place of the sinner. And that is precisely what Jesus has done. He frees us not only from the guilt and slavery of sin, but also from the anger which our sins justly deserve.

## Guilt-feelings

Guilt is not a specifically Christian problem. It is a human problem. Jean-Baptiste Clamence, in Camus' story *The Fall*, is plagued by guilt. He once witnessed a young woman commit suicide by jumping into the Seine from the Pont Royal. He did nothing to save her. He feels his hypocrisy is exposed, and from then on a feeling of guilt rarely leaves him. Years later, on board an ocean liner, he thinks he sees a drowning person in the sea and he panics. It turns out to be a false alarm, but it brings home to him the inescapability of his own guilt:

'Then I realised calmly, just as you resign yourself to an idea the truth of which you have long known, that that cry which had sounded over the Seine behind me years before had never ceased, carried by the river to the waters of the Channel, to travel throughout the world, across the limitless expanse of the Ocean, and that it had waited for me there until the day I encountered it. I realised likewise that it would continue to await me on seas and rivers, everywhere, in short, where lies the bitter water of my baptism'.[3]

Before we can deal with guilt personally we must discover an important distinction: that between guilt and guilt-feelings. Guilt is our legal state after breaking a law. Guilt-feelings are composed of a variety of emotions - shame over what one has done, anxiety in anticipation of being punished and grief for loss of self-esteem. What confuses the issue is that most people today use the word 'guilt' when they really mean guilt-feeling. In addition these guilt-feelings are almost invariably thought of as something bad. As we shall see, this is by no means necessarily so.

## Four Possible Situations

The first possibility is exhibited in the Bible by Adam, Judas and Governor Felix. It is possible to have guilt-feelings when we are guilty. Indeed it is most likely that we will. When Adam disobeyed God, he felt guilty and he hid from God. When Judas betrayed Jesus, he felt guilt and remorse and he committed suicide. When Felix heard Paul speak of righteousness, self-control and judgement to come, he felt guilt and fear - and with good reason, because, as the Roman historian Tacitus says 'with savagery and lust he exercised the powers of a king with the disposition of a slave'.[4] In all these cases it is right and proper that the person should feel guilt. He *is* guilty, morally guilty.

Secondly, it is possible that we might not feel guilty when in fact we are guilty. Joseph's brothers, David and Simon the Pharisee come into this category. Joseph's older brothers (except Reuben) sold Joseph into slavery and deceived their father into thinking he was dead, all apparently without a twinge of conscience, until they were themselves in trouble in Egypt. Similarly David, after committing adultery with Bathsheba and having her husband killed, did not appear to be bothered by a guilty conscience, until the prophet Nathan said, 'Thou art the man!' Neither is there any indication that Simon the Pharisee felt guilty at his shameful treatment of Jesus, even when shown up by the example of the 'sinful woman'. The lack of guilt-feelings in these instances is not a strength but a glaring weakness.

Jesus' disciples picking corn on the Sabbath (Matthew 12:1-8), Mary anointing Jesus (John 12:1-8) and Peter in Antioch (Galatians 2:12) may all illustrate the third possibility - guilt-feelings when there is no guilt. Both the disciples and Mary may have felt guilty when their conduct was challenged by authoritative people, so that Jesus felt obliged to declare their innocence. Peter's case is even more serious. His mistaken feeling of guilt actually led him to commit sin! When the legalists came down from Jerusalem, he felt guilty about his eating with Gentiles, and, as a result, ate separately with fellow Jews, thus breaking the unity of the church. Guilt-feelings that have no connection with a real guilt are very destructive.

Of course there is another possibility - a clear conscience when innocent. The supreme example of that is Jesus himself. 'Can any of you prove me guilty of sin?' he challenged his opponents (John 8:46). He had no consciousness of sin in himself, because he had done no wrong. But can anyone else have a clear conscience? Can an ordinary sinful man be innocent? Astonishingly, the Bible says yes! Jesus called his disciples innocent (Matthew 12:7). He did not mean by that they were sinless, but that with regard to the particular question of Sabbath-breaking they were blameless. He implies, therefore, that they could have a clear conscience. This is put beyond doubt by the Apostle Paul. Speaking before the Sanhedrin he claims, 'I have fulfilled my duty to God in all good conscience to this day'. He did not mean by this, and by similar statements in his epistles, that he was sinless, but that with regard to the particular duty of proclaiming the gospel, he had a good conscience. It is entirely possible, then, to have a clear conscience. Indeed, that is what we should all be aiming at (1 Timothy 1:5, 1 Peter 3:16).

### Feeling guilty?

So how should we deal with guilt-feelings? The answer depends entirely on whether we are actually morally guilty or not. If we are morally guilty of breaking God's law (not merely man-made laws) then our real moral guilt must be dealt with. It's no good trying to deal merely with the guilt-feelings by telling yourself to cheer up, or by pretending you have not really done wrong, or by getting drunk, or by getting psychiatric help (only). There is only one way in which real guilt can be removed and that is through the punishment of the offence. If we bore the punishment of our offence against God, it would mean hell for us. But, as we have seen, the message of Christian liberation is that Jesus bore the punishment of our offence upon the cross. He suffered there the shame and the misery and the alienation from God that is rightly ours. All that is required of us is that we recognise our guilt and that we plead for (and therefore certainly receive) forgiveness through the redeeming death of Jesus Christ (see Luke 18:13 and Ephesians 1:7).

What should we do when we are plagued by guilt-feelings, either vague or specific? If these bear no relation to any offence against God's law, there is only one answer. We must educate our consciences. This is precisely what Jesus does in the cornfield and in Bethany and what Paul does in Antioch. They make clear the particular behaviour in question is not sinful at all. Those who were trying to make others feel guilty are wrong. Consciences have to be brought into line with God's commands not with the guilt-mongers' dictates.

## *Three Consciences*

Our consciences have to be trained, just as dogs have to be trained. I grew up on a sheep farm in the North of Scotland. We always had several sheepdogs - Border Collies - all the shepherds had. For the most part they were reasonably well trained (the dogs, that is, although the shepherds weren't bad either!) but occasionally you would come across a dog that had been cruelly treated, or a dog that had been allowed to run wild. Consciences can be like that too. There is the conscience that is dominated by legalism. It is like the dog that has been chained up, starved and beaten. It is terrified of putting a foot out of line, with the result that it is useless. The legalist conscience begins with the idea that you can be saved through keeping the law of God perfectly and ends up adding masses of manmade rules to God's law, because you can never be sure that you are doing enough. The legalist conscience is terrified of enjoying anything. This is the conscience that has often passed for the Christian conscience. But that is a deception. It is the conscience of the Pharisee, not of the Nazarene.

Then there is the conscience that is spoiled by licence. It is like the dog that is allowed to do anything, either because it is indulged or because it is neglected. The dog may chase cars, bite postmen or worry sheep. The conscience will condone any conduct as long as it is enjoyable, no matter how transient or destructive the pleasure. This is the conscience that twentieth century man has craved - a conscience free from law, free from any moral absolute, but he has found only another slavery. Jimi Hendrix, the vastly talented rock musician who died tragically in 1970, said, 'If I'm free its because I'm always running'. Running away or always running towards some new dream can become just another addiction. And there is a frightening rebound effect. The conscience that has no absolute law to guide it can run wild and start to accuse you of anything, leading to the formation of all kinds of guilt complexes.

The Christian conscience is the one that knows true liberty. It is like the sheepdog running free on the hill under his master's eye. The sheepdog knows his purpose in life, he knows his master's commands, he knows his master's love. Likewise the Christian knows real freedom within the scope of his Master's law and love. He is like a footballer playing within the rules of the game and the instructions of his manager. James speaks of 'the perfect law that gives freedom'(James 1:25) and Paul says, 'It is for freedom that Christ has set us free. Stand firm, then, and do not let yourselves be burdened again by a yoke of slavery . . . . You, my brothers, were called to be free. But do not use your freedom to indulge the sinful nature; rather serve one another in love. The entire law is summed up in a single command: "'Love your neighbour as yourself'". Christian liberty is the perfect balance between the extremes of legalism and licence. It is a balance of liberty within the law, a balance of form and freedom.

## Lord of Creation

Christianity is often conceived of as something narrow and restrictive. Nothing could be further from the truth. It is the legalist imitation that is narrow and restrictive. Christianity is as wide as the universe of its Lord. The universe was created by Christ and for Christ (Colossians 1:16). He is the King of kings and the Lord of all. Man was created as his viceroy to have dominion over the creatures (Genesis 1:26). God 'crowned him with glory and honour and put everything under his feet' (Psalm 8:6). Yet, at the Fall, mankind failed and the creation was no longer manageable (Genesis 3:17-19). This is the problem the writer to the Hebrews recognises after quoting Psalm 8, but he has an answer:

> In putting everything under him (man), God left nothing that is not subject to him. Yet at present we do not see everything subject to him. But we see Jesus, who was made a little lower than the angels, now crowned with glory and honour because he suffered death, so that by the grace of God he might taste death for everyone (Hebrews 2:8,9).

The Son of God, through incarnation and death, has taken to himself the human lordship over creation as well as the divine. The universe is governed by one man, the man Christ Jesus, and 'he must reign until he has put all his enemies under his feet' (1 Corinthians 15:25). The question is not whether Christ has authority over any particular area, but whether you are for him or against him in that particular area. If you are for him, 'all things are yours, whether Paul or Apollos or Cephas or the world or life or death or the present or the future' (1 Corinthians 3:21,22).

Christ is the Lord of the whole of life and there is no

area of life that is out of bounds for the Christian, except what is sinful in itself. One of the greatest mistakes in the history of Christianity is the division of life into the sacred and the secular. If, as the New Testament teaches, the Christian's body is the temple of the Holy Spirit, then every matter of human interest is sacred, whether physical, psychological, social or spiritual. Science, industry, cultural activities, politics and communication media are all open to the Christian, and not just as ways of making a living, or of 'spoiling the Egyptians' as it is sometimes quaintly put, but as areas of significance in themselves, areas where the Lordship of Christ must be recognised.

CHAPTER 10
# FREEDOM FROM ADDICTION

All sin is addictive. Jesus said, 'Everyone who sins is a slave to sin' (John 8:34). But some sins are more obviously addictive than others. Especially sins with a strong physiological component, such as sexual sins or alcohol and drug abuse, appear extremely addictive. In this chapter I wish to look at alcohol and drug abuse in particular.

## *Alcohol*

Alcohol is a chemical. Its chemical name is ethanol. It is formed by a natural process of fermentation. For instance, when grapes are crushed, and the enzymes in the skin come in contact with the sugars in the fruit, alcohol is formed. Alcohol is a chemical that can be absorbed by the body. All our food and drink is made up of chemicals of one kind or another. And each of these chemicals can either help us or harm us. For one thing, the effect depends on the amount of the chemical we take. For instance we can kill ourselves if we take excessive amounts of sugar or salt over long periods.

Sugar is a good example. If we are tired and hungry and we take something containing sugar, it makes us feel better almost immediately. This is because our blood-sugar level was low and so we lacked energy. The intake of sugar has helped us. But we all know that if we eat too much sugar, we cause problems. Our teeth decay. We get overweight. We strain our hearts. Eating too much sugar can kill us eventually.

This is also true of alcohol, which of course is much more potent in its effects than sugar! And we don't need alcohol to live whereas we do need sugar, or carbohydrate in some form. When alcohol is taken it goes straight into the bloodstream and has an immediate effect on the brain. The parts of the brain that control and to some extent inhibit behaviour are made less effective by alcohol. This can make a person more talkative and outgoing. But alcohol also impairs the senses, physical co-ordination, memory and concentration. The more alcohol that is drunk, the worse these effects become, until a person's behaviour becomes so unreasonable and clumsy that he is termed 'drunk'. Eventually, if sufficient alcohol is taken, the drinker will become unconscious or even die from paralysis of centres controlling the vital functions of breathing, swallowing and circulation.

Regular excessive drinking results in lasting damage. Ultimately, heavy drinkers find that they cannot do without alcohol (it is more addictive than cocaine). It becomes almost impossible to give it up, as any lessening of intake will result in horrible withdrawal symptoms. These may include convulsions, terrifying hallucinations and coma. In addition excessive drinking causes many other problems. The health problems range from obesity and nutritional deficiencies to cirrhosis of the liver, brain damage and heart disease. Alcohol abuse also results in public and domestic violence, road traffic accidents, divorce and homelessness.

## Society and Alcohol Abuse

How great a problem is alcohol abuse in our society today? The amount of alcohol consumed in Scotland has doubled in the last twenty years. As a nation we are spending £3.5 million a day on drink - more than we spend on clothes or travelling. Convictions for drinking and driving rose from 3,536 in 1963 to 11,557 in 1983. Half of the drivers killed on our roads have blood alcohol levels in excess of 80mg% ('the legal limit'). Alcohol abuse is now the main killer of the under 25's. One in five men admitted to hospital is there with an alcohol-related problem.

How has society viewed the problem? And how have we gone about tackling it? Until quite recently, the prevailing view in medical circles, and therefore in society at large, was that a certain type of person was at risk from alcohol, while the rest of the population could consume large quantities without becoming addicted or causing serious problems. It was thought that some people were prone to be 'alcoholics', while others were not, no matter how much they drank. Linked to this idea was the use of the term 'alcoholism' to describe what was thought of as a distinct disease or illness.

As a result of this view, the alcohol industry was able to argue that increasing consumption of their product would do no harm to the vast majority of people. Of course, there were the unfortunate minority who were predisposed to alcoholism and who should be treated for their illness. This is the position which has been accepted by successive governments, with the result that no action has been taken to curb the growth of alcohol consumption.

## Change of View

However, this whole view has now been proved false. The medical profession has dropped the term 'alcoholism' in favour of 'alcohol abuse'. It is now recognised that anyone who drinks excessively is in serious danger of becoming addicted to alcohol and of permanently damaging his health. It has also been shown that the less alcohol costs (in real terms) the more alcohol is consumed. And the more alcohol is consumed, the more alcohol-related problems we have.

It is clear, therefore, that we must find some way of reducing the present dangerously high level of alcohol consumption in our society. There are two possible ways of doing this - educating the public to drink less or increasing the cost of alcohol. There is the third possibility of total prohibition, but that was tried in America earlier this century and it failed miserably, because the law was felt to be unjust and it was broken indiscriminately.

All attempts to educate the public about the dangers of excessive drinking and to encourage a sensible attitude to alcohol are worthwhile and the Bible has much to teach us on the subject, as we shall see. There is far too much mystique about alcohol, far too much ignorance and far too much nonsense. Still, it is the Government who can take the most effective action to reduce alcohol abuse, simply by increasing the cost of alcohol. It has been proved that even small increases in the cost leads to a reduction in consumption, abuse and alcohol-related problems. But the alcohol industry is very powerful and influential with governments, and it certainly does not want consumption (and therefore profits) to fall.

## *The Bible and Alcohol*

What attitude should Christians have to alcohol in light of the dangerously high level of alcohol abuse today? We must have a responsible attitude, but our views will not be formulated only by the contemporary situation. As in every other question of belief or behaviour, we must get our principles from God's Word. What does the Bible have to say about alcohol? Basically it has two things to say. Wine is a good gift of God and drunkenness is a sin. Any Christian view of alcohol has to take account of both principles.

In view of the problems caused by alcohol abuse, we might want to say that no-one should drink alcohol. But the Bible will not allow us to say that. Wine is portrayed in the Bible as a benefit. God gives wine that gladdens the heart of man (Psalm 104:15). The blessings of the gospel are figuratively described as wine (Isaiah 55:1). Wine was a necessary part of the offerings to God (Leviticus 23:13). Jesus turned water into wine for the celebration of a wedding (John 2:9) and he made wine part of the celebration of the Lord's Supper (Matthew 26:27-29). Incidentally, the various words for wine in the Bible all describe alcoholic drinks, as each word is sometimes used in the context of drunkenness. And anyway the process of fermentation sets in immediately grapes are crushed.

On the other hand, drunkenness is clearly condemned in the Bible. It is a sin (among other sins) that excludes someone from the kingdom of God, unless repented of (1 Corinthians 6:10,11). It led, in the cases of Noah and Lot, to other sins (Genesis 9:21 and 19:33). But the passage that describes most clearly the effects of drunkenness itself is Proverbs 23:29-35. The misery of hangovers, hallucinations and addiction are all there.

Alcohol is a drug. It produces a sense of euphoria or well-being (it gladdens the heart of man). And it appears to be the only drug that is permitted in the Bible for non-medicinal purposes (it is also permitted for medicinal purposes - 1 Timothy 5:23). Just as Jesus' presence at the wedding in Cana shows he approves of marriage, so his miracle shows he approves of wine. Alcohol is like every other thing in the created world. It may be used for good or evil. Just as the attraction of man for woman may be good (marriage) or evil (adultery), so the use of alcohol may be good (celebration) or evil (drunkenness).

It might be concluded that as long as a person does not become drunk, then it is all right to drink alcohol. That indeed is the base line. But there are two other factors to be considered. For the Christian at least, harming one's body is wrong, because it is the temple of the Holy Spirit (1 Corinthians 6:19). So drinking enough to damage one's body is wrong, even although one is not obviously drunk.

In addition we must consider the effect of our actions on others: we must not lead anyone else into sin (Romans 14:21). Sometimes we ought to impose voluntary limitations on our own Christian liberty for the sake of others. For this reason many Christians today will only drink wine at communion, abstaining completely at other times. Other Christians, equally concerned for the good of others, seek to give a good example of how to use alcohol wisely. They will drink alcohol infrequently and only in small amounts.

## Alcohol Use or Non-use

There are, really, only these two options for the Christian (or for anyone else concerned for their own welfare and that of others). We may decide not to drink alcohol at all (except at the Lord's Supper), or we may decide to drink only in moderation.

If we choose not to drink, that is not the end of our problems. We live in a society where alcohol is widely used (and abused). We may be tempted, even pressurised, to drink. So we must be very clear on our reasons for not drinking, and be prepared to state them courteously when necessary. We must also work out a Christian attitude to drinkers. We must respect those who use alcohol responsibly and moderately. In particular, we must not view Christians who drink as second class. Nor should we laugh or sneer at people who get drunk. Drunkenness is a sin. We should have compassion on others who sin, just as God, in Christ, has had compassion on us.

If we do decide to drink, we must bear in mind the serious dangers of drinking too much, and we must be sure we are not drinking for the wrong reasons. Let us take the wrong reasons first. We should not drink just to be like everyone else, to show off, to forget our problems, or to be 'a man'. If these are our reasons, we will feel great pressure to drink too much - just to be like others, to show off, to forget our problems, or to be 'a man'. The Bible indicates that right reasons for drinking wine are - to celebrate, to aid social occasions and to gladden the heart. Drinking too much does not serve these purposes.

To make clear what is meant by 'drinking too much' it is necessary to explain what a unit of alcohol is. This is the expression used to describe one standard drink - a half pint of beer, a small measure of spirits, a glass of wine, or a small glass of sherry. The Scottish Council on Alcohol and the Scottish Health Education Group recommend as sensible limits 4 to 6 units of alcohol no more than two or three times a week for men, and half that amount for women. But they stress that even these amounts may be dangerous - for example, before driving or operating machinery, or if a woman is pregnant. The Christian would also question the justification for drinking that amount as frequently as indicated, even in financial terms alone.

Also, you must remember that alcohol affects your judgement, including your judgement of how alcohol is affecting you. So if you do decide to drink, then it is wise to decide beforehand how much you are going to drink, say one pint of beer or two glasses of wine, and then stick to that limit.

Again, the Christian who decides to use alcohol responsibly must have a right attitude to those who do not drink. He should not look down on them as wet-blankets or spoilsports, nor should he try to undermine their conscience in this matter. There ought to be a mutual recognition of Christian freedom.

## Hope for the Alcoholic?

So far we have discussed ways of preventing addiction to alcohol. And it must be said that in this area, as in many others, prevention is better than cure. But what of the alcoholic, the person who has become addicted to alcohol? Is there any hope for him or for her? It must be said that there is very little hope. That is not being unkind or unduly pessimistic. It is just facing facts. The long-term recovery rate is alarmingly small. But that is not the same as saying there is no hope for the alcoholic. There is no hope for any of us, except by the grace of God. But the grace of God is sufficient for our weakness, whatever our weakness may be.

There were alcoholics in the church at Corinth. Paul mentions drunkards in his list of sinners that are excluded from the kingdom of God. But then he says, 'And that is what some of you were. But you were washed, you were sanctified, you were justified in the name of the Lord Jesus Christ and by the Spirit of our God' (1 Corinthians 6:11). So there is hope for the alcoholic, the same hope there is for any of us, the hope of being saved by Jesus Christ. So we should do as much as we can to help people with alcohol problems, though it will often be a thankless task. Jesus was not afraid to be a friend of sinners, even although people slandered him as drunkard for it (Luke 7:34).

## Drugs

What exactly do we mean by 'drugs'? In its more general use 'drug' simply means a medicine, but the drugs that are misused are what we call 'psycho-active' drugs. These act on the brain and alter a person's emotions or mental state. There is a great variation in the effects and dangers of various drugs. A distinction is also made between 'legal' and 'illegal' drugs. Drugs which are legally available range from caffeine (in tea, coffee and many soft drinks) to nicotine and alcohol. We have already considered alcohol and it is particularly illegal drugs which we will look at now, but it is worth remembering that tobacco contributes to at least 100,000 premature deaths in the UK every year.

Before we look at specific illegal drugs, it will be useful to understand some terms used to describe certain effects of psycho-active drugs. *Tolerance* refers to the way the body usually adapts to the repeated use of a drug, meaning that it takes higher doses to maintain the same effect. *Withdrawal symptoms* occur when the regular use of some drugs is reduced or stopped - usually a few hours after the last use. These symptoms may be like an extemely severe attack of 'flu' and be accompanied by hallucinations, delirium and fits. *Dependence* describes a compulsion to continue taking a drug as a result of its repeated use. If this is to avoid the discomfort of withdrawal, it is called physical dependence. If it is simply for the stimulating or pleasant effects of the drug, it is called psychological dependence.

## Four Groups of Drugs

There are four general groups of drugs - depressants, stimulants, hallucinogens and solvents. Depressants include heroin, morphine, barbiturates, tranquillisers and cannabis. The term 'depressant' is used because all these

drugs depress brain activity giving feelings of well-being
and relaxation. One of the most dangerous depressants is
heroin. At first it relieves stress and discomfort, but once
the user becomes dependent he must increase the dose
just to feel 'normal'. In reality all his bodily functions slow
down and he becomes extremely apathetic, but he is
deterred from stopping the drug because of the fear of
withdrawal pains.

Barbiturates and tranquillisers may, of course, like
most other drugs, be quite legally prescribed by doctors.
However, it is now recognised that barbiturates are very
dangerous drugs. Both overdose and sudden withdrawal
can be fatal. It has also been discovered that long-term
use of tranquillisers, even at therapeutic dosages leads to
tolerance, dependence and withdrawal effects such as
insomnia, anxiety and nausea.

Stimulants are similar to depressants in that they give a
feeling of euphoria, but they differ in that this is accompanied not by relaxation but by exhilaration and increased
energy. The main stimulants that are misused illegally are
cocaine and amphetamines. The prolonged use of both
these drugs leads to psychological dependence, and
heavy use will lead to mental illness.

The best known hallucinogen is LSD (also known as a
psychedelic drug). These drugs are dangerous, not
because they produce physical dependence but because
their effects are unpredictable. They may cause hallucinations and confusion (rather like a delirium experienced by
young children with a high temperature). LSD is taken for
the hallucinatory effects, which are often conceived of as
mystical or ecstatic experiences. However, the user may
experience depression, disorientation and panic ('a bad
trip'), and death by accident is a possibility as the user is
not perceiving the real world.

Cannabis (marihuana) too is sometimes known as a
psychedelic drug, because with high doses there may be
perceptual distortion, but it is also a depressant like alcohol. It produces a strong psychological dependence in
some users, and people chronically intoxicated on

cannabis appear apathetic and sluggish.

A very worrying trend in recent years has been the abuse of solvents by some young people. These are not controlled drugs, and are widely used in a great variety of industrial and domestic products. Inhaling or 'sniffing' the vapours of these solvents can be extremely dangerous. While the desired effect is a happy or euphoric state, this may be followed by confusion, seizures or unconsciousness, or even death.

## *Why Drug Abuse?*

If most drugs are clearly so dangerous, why do so many people abuse drugs? There is no easy answer to that question, but the main factors are ignorance (or unconcern) of the danger, cheapness and availability of the drug, curiosity and pleasure in the user, along with more complex reasons such as rebellion against authority and attraction to the mysterious.

However, most of these factors have always existed. Why is it in the second half of the twentieth century that drug abuse has escalated so alarmingly in the western world? I think there are two reasons - a change in our view of man and the formation of a youth culture.

Until relatively recently it was generally accepted that man was the crown of God's creation, a creature with purpose, dignity and responsibility. But now man is seen as 'a naked ape', a chemical machine, 'a chance collocation of atoms'. It is little wonder that young people raised on such pseudo-scientific platitudes should turn to drugs as a chemical answer to their problems. C.S. Lewis pointed out the irony in this modern situation when he wrote, 'We laugh at honour and are shocked to find traitors in our midst. We castrate and bid the geldings be fruitful'.[1]

Secondly, the '50s and '60s gave birth to what can be called a distinctive youth culture. There were many factors in this. We can look at only one - rock music. Whatever the merits of the music itself, there is no doubt that the lifestyles of the singers and bands, and the lyrics of the songs have greatly influenced young people.

Drugs, of course, had been part of the music scene in the USA long before the birth of rock music, but with the increasing awareness of the emptiness of contemporary life many more musicians turned to drugs. They had the money to finance their 'habits', and they had the perfect medium to communicate their ideas to others. All this reached a climax with the psychedelic music and 'acid rock' of the late '60s. But the utopian dreams of 'the Woodstock generation' foundered with the deaths by overdoses of Jimi Hendrix and Janis Joplin in 1970. The idea that drugs could create a new world was largely abandoned. Nevertheless, the threshold of the acceptability of drugs was permanently lowered, and drug-taking became an escape from harsh reality.

## Christianity and Drugs

Is there a distinctively Christian view of drugs? There is no specific biblical passage that deals with the subject, but there are some general principles that are relevant. First, our bodies are temples of the Holy Spirit (1 Corinthians 6:19) and ought not to be despised or abused. Second, we ought not to take drugs to blot out reality, because that is part of the sin of drunkenness, and anyway, reality is God's reality. When Jesus was offered a drugged drink before crucifixion, he refused (Mark 15:23). Third, we are to obey the civil ruler (Romans 13:1-7), unless he commands us to do what God forbids, or forbids us to do what God commands (Acts 5:29). Therefore, if the law requires that controlled drugs can only be used by doctor's prescription, we must obey that law.

What about those who abuse drugs? Is there any hope for those who become addicted? I want to answer that by telling the story of someone who illustrates many of the things I've mentioned. He started recording for the legendary Sun Records, Memphis, along with Elvis Presley, Carl Perkins and Jerry Lee Lewis. He went on to become one of the greatest singers of American Country music.

His name is Johnny Cash.[2]

Like many other musicians of the time he started taking amphetamines, discovering that, at first, they seemed to bring expanded limits to his stamina and performing ability. They also helped to quieten his conscience - for a time. Soon he was addicted. His singing deteriorated. He broke engagements. He became erratic, frenzied and unapproachable. In seven years, he wrecked every car he owned, two jeeps, two tractors and a bulldozer, escaping death several times only by inches. But it wasn't only vehicles he smashed up. More tragically, his marriage too broke under the strain. He was jailed seven times, the last time in October 1967.

That was when he admitted for the first time in his life that he was all wrong and he couldn't free himself. He needed help, especially God's help. Surrounded by praying friends, he went through the horror of withdrawal from the combined addiction to amphetamines and barbiturates - the waking nightmare of feeling slivers of glass pouring through his veins, and thorns and worms tearing his flesh. By the grace of God he came through. And a major factor in his recovery was that he recognised that drug addiction wasn't his only problem. Bound up with it were pride, arrogance and deception, of which he had to repent. Since that time he has been a committed Christian.

The story of Johnny Cash proves that there is hope in the gospel even for the drug addict, but for every recovered addict there are thousands who die in misery.

## CHAPTER 11
# CHIMES OF FREEDOM

Rock music has been largely about the pursuit of freedom. The images of longing, yearning, running, breaking free and feeling free are legion. The freedom of the open road, freedom in sexual relationships, political freedom, psychologial or spiritual freedom through the use of drugs, music or mystical religion - they're all there. Mostly it's the longing for freedom that's there, not freedom itself, from Chuck Berry's 'The Promised Land' to Dylan's 'Chimes of Freedom' to Springsteen's 'Hungry Heart'. The history of rock music, perhaps better than anything else in the modern world, illustrates St Augustine's dictum, 'Man was made for God, and his heart is forever restless until it finds rest in him'.

## *The Devil's Music?*

This raises the whole question of whether this longing for freedom is the kind of thing the Christian should be interested in. Surely the Christian has found true freedom in Christ, it is argued. He doesn't need Rock 'n' Roll's version. Indeed, some go so far as to say rock is positively dangerous. The most celebrated (or vilified, depending on your point of view) attempt in this direction in recent years has been *Pop goes the Gospel* by John Blanchard.[1] In fact, the same approach was taken years earlier in the States by Frank Garlock, Bob Larson and others. These writers are saying, in effect, 'Rock musicians are obsessed with sex, drugs, violence and the occult, and here are examples from their lives. Rock lyrics are about sex, drugs, violence and the occult, and here are quotations to prove it. Rock music is too loud and repetitive. Therefore, Christians should have nothing to do with it'.

I do not doubt that John Blanchard is writing out of the best of motives. He is rightly concerned about Christian young people unthinkingly swallowing whatever rock music dishes up. He is also rightly concerned about the undiscerning use of rock music in evangelism. And he is rightly concerned about the world-imitating drivel of what sometimes passes as Christian rock music. But unfortunately, anyone who has even a passing acquaintance with a wide variety of rock music and other areas of modern life cannot really take the main argument of *Pop goes the Gospel* seriously.

As Steve Turner comments on the writings of Larson and Blanchard in his well-researched and excellently written book *Hungry for Heaven*:

'These men tend to extract the worst behaviour of known performers and use it to generalise about rock 'n' roll as a whole, rather like detailing the sexual preferences of a fallen TV evangelist to explain what's wrong with preaching today. Often, in fact, their information is completely wrong (like saying Black Sabbath held black masses "on stage" or that part of *Goat's Head Soup* by the Rolling Stones was recorded at a voodoo ritual) and they indiscriminately quote musicians talking the inanest rubbish, believing it to be authoritative because it supports their argument'.[2]

Their arguments are reminiscent of a man who once tried to prove to me that all art forms are illegitimate for the Christian. He argued: the greatest art form is the play, Hamlet is the greatest play, Hamlet is not Christian, therefore all art is illegitimate for the Christian! With equal logic I could argue: the greatest art form is the song, the Twenty-third Psalm is the greatest song, the Twenty-third Psalm is Christian, therefore all art forms are Christian! To say that some rock music is pornographic, therefore Christians should steer clear of rock music, is like saying that some magazines are pornographic, therefore Christians should steer clear of magazines. The truth is that all art forms can be abused for sinful purposes.

But what about the argument that there is something about the form of rock music itself that is incompatible with Christianity? I believe it can be legitimately argued that some art forms are incompatible with Christianity, just as it can be argued that some sports are incompatible with Christianity. It can be argued convincingly that John Cage's chance music is incompatible with Christianity, or that surrealism is incompatible with Christianity, just as it can be argued that bull-fighting or bear-baiting is incompatible with Christianity: the sports, because they can be deemed immoral in that they exploit the sufferings of our fellow creatures for our entertainment and financial gain; the art forms, because, in themselves, they present a different world view from Christianity. Can it similarly be argued that the musical *genre* of rock 'n' roll is incompatible with Christianity because its form basically contradicts the Christian world view or Christian morality? To answer that question we must first try to answer another - what is rock 'n' roll?

## Rock Roots

Garlock, Larson and Blanchard & Co say rock is essentially loud, repetitious music whose basic rhythms have a mainly sexual effect on its hearers. This sounds very plausible and is, no doubt, an accurate description of a lot of *pop* music. But the trouble is, it is both too general and too specific to be a definition of rock music: too general because it covers most kinds of dance music down through the ages, and too specific because it covers only some kinds of rock music. Now if these writers wish to warn against the dangers of certain types of dance music, OK, I will go along with a great deal of what they have to say. But it is specifically their wrong definition of rock music that I object to. Rock music is not essentially dance music. In fact it can be shown that the overall effect of rock music has been to stop people dancing and to get them to listen to the music. The usual venue for live rock music is not the dance hall but the theatre or the stadium. Millions of people listen to rock music at home, in the car or walking along the street, and few of them seem to have an irresistible urge to get up and dance all the time! And when people do dance to rock music they generally do it not as couples but as individuals, or as whole crowds in spontaneous free expression. There is no doubt that rock music has a power and a great attraction. But to understand it we must delve deeper.

There is general agreement that rock 'n' roll originated in the American South in the early Fifties and that the prototype rock 'n' roller was Elvis Presley. Although it may have appeared that rock 'n' roll came out of the blue like a clap of thunder, no music does that. Every musical form has roots. The roots of rock 'n' roll lie in three separate musical traditions - blues, gospel and country. Steve Turner explains it like this:

> 'Rock 'n' roll, as a commercial music aimed at white teenagers, was born in the Southern States of America, where the predominant religion was Protestant non-conformism and the musical heritage a mixture of Celtic folk, English hymns and West African rhythm. The founding fathers of rock 'n' roll, men born in the immediate pre-war years, were touched by each of these'.[3]

The 'founding fathers' were people like Jerry Lee Lewis, Chuck Berry, Little Richard, Buddy Holly and above all Elvis Presley. The songs on Elvis's first single have a strong claim to being the first Southern rock 'n' roll record of all. On one side was the country bluegrass song 'Blue Moon of Kentucky' and on the other the blues song 'That's all right'. Not only did these songs come from different backgrounds - the first from hillbilly folk music and the second from black blues music - but Elvis performed the first with a blues feel and the second with a jaunty country beat. The third tributary of rock 'n' roll, gospel, comes through in the intensity of emotional power in the singing of the best rock. Of course these three tributaries, blues, gospel and country, are themselves amalgams of other influences - black spirituals and working songs, European (especially Celtic) folk song and English hymnody.

But there is one essential ingredient of the recipe for rock which we haven't yet mentioned, and it is the most obvious - the beat. Rock 'n' roll did not invent the beat. It was there already in rhythm & blues (R & B) and in some country music. Rock took it over and made it one of its distinctive elements. But what is its significance? The cliche is that it has sexual overtones. But that simply does not explain why the distinctive rhythm is there in all kinds of rock songs whether the theme is sexual or not (and some of the greatest rock songs have not been sexual in theme - 'Like a Rolling Stone' or 'Born in the USA'). The real significance of the rhythm, I suspect, is that rock music is essentially city music. It reflects the sounds, the rhythms, the trains, the cars, above all the urgency of city life.

This urgency is one indispensable ingredient of rock music. The others are the plaintive yearning of the blues, the emotional power of gospel or soul music and the sheer acoustic power of electrical amplification. Put all these together and you have enormous potential for the resolution of musical tensions, not only in the standard twelve or sixteen bar chordal patterns which rock has inherited from blues or country, but also in the interweaving pattern of relentless driving rhythm with soaring vocals or instrumentals.

All that urgency and power and tension can of course be abused, as it so often has been abused, for immoral purposes. But that is not what rock music is *per se*. Rock music is about the struggles, the unbearable tensions, the cries from the heart and the longings for glory and freedom of late twentieth century man. To illustrate that we will look at two of the most influential figures in the rock music of the last three decades - Bob Dylan and Bruce Springsteen. I am well aware that, in selecting them, I am concentrating on what may be called serious rock music. I make no apology. Too often rock has been presented, both by its friends and by its enemies, as mindless noise. Equally, I am concentrating on rock music with a rough, raw edge. Neither Dylan nor Springsteen are smooth, sweet pop, by any stretch of the imagination. But that too is part of what rock music is at its best. It does not pretend that the world is all sweetness and light. There is bitterness and darkness too.

## Folk to Rock

Dylan, more than any other individual, realised the full potential of rock 'n' roll and, in doing so, changed its direction. This is how Stephen Barnard, writing in *The Encyclopedia of Rock*, estimates Dylan's impact on rock:

'Never one to simply follow trends, Dylan's great contribution to rock was to explore surprising new avenues and extend the music's frame of reference - not once but several times . . . . He changed the very nature of the pop song, eschewing its traditional subject matter . . . . He took social and political comment into the record charts for the first time and introduced a new realism into rock lyrics. He changed the language of pop songwriting, making brilliant use of literary devices like irony and metaphor and bringing a poetic quality to songs'.[4]

A teenager in the classic rock 'n' roll years of the fifties, he formed several groups in his home town in Minnesota, singing Little Richard style, but, with the faltering of the impetus of rock, he (along with many others) turned back to the roots in folk and blues, especially the music of Woody Guthrie. It was when he came to New York and wrote his own songs about contemporary social and political concerns that he began to have a national and then an international impact in the early Sixties - songs like 'Blowing in the Wind', 'Masters of War' and 'The Times They Are A-Changin''. The recurring theme of those songs was freedom - freedom from racial prejudice, war and injustice: 'How many years can some people exist /Before they're allowed to be free'?[5]

For a while Dylan was a figurehead of the Civil Rights movement, but he became disillusioned with that. He felt there was a deeper freedom to be discovered at a more personal level. That longing emerges in songs like 'Chimes of Freedom': 'And we gazed upon the chimes of freedom flashing'.[6] He was disillusioned with the preachy, finger-pointing style of the Movement. He wasn't sure any more of values and standards he'd taken for granted before. The freedom that was opening up before him now was a total freedom, a freedom from all restrictions. He was moving into a world without maps, without land-marks. In 'My Back Pages' he speaks of this move from a world of absolutes to a world of relativism: 'Ah, but I was so much older then /I'm younger than that now'.[7]

Dylan understood that modern existentialist thought had no moral categories. There was no right and wrong, no good and bad. The only reality was your own experi-ence, your own feelings, your own decision to be free. Around that time (1964) a renaissance of rock music was taking place in Britain through the Beatles, the Rolling Stones and others. The Beatles especially were influenced by Dylan's songs, but the Beatles in turn showed Dylan that rock was a vibrant musical form again. In particular, it didn't have all the restrictions of the Civil Rights, folk song scene. Dylan's move back into the rock idiom signalled the start of one of the most prolific and influential periods of his career. In fourteen months he created the three albums, *Bringing It All Back Home, Highway 61 Revisited* and *Blonde on Blonde*, which were to alter the face of rock music. He combined the folk emphasis on thoughtful lyrics with the emotional power of R & B and Chuck Berry style rock 'n' roll.

The songs of these albums explore love, hate, alien-ation, absurdity, but most of all, there is that longing for freedom which I have suggested is intrinsic to rock 'n' roll. This ranges from the longing for freedom from the restric-tions and stupidity of society in 'Subterranean Homesick Blues', 'Maggie's Farm', 'It's Alright Ma (I'm Only Bleeding)' and 'Desolation Row', to the longing for the freedom of some personal, psychological paradise in 'Mr Tambourine Man', 'Gates of Eden' and 'Visions of Johanna'. But the more this total freedom is pursued, the more there is an alienation from other people and a feeling of gloomy fore-boding. He speaks of 'Waiting to find out what price /You have to pay to get out of /Going through all these things twice'.[8]   'Like a Rolling Stone', named by *New Musical Express* in 1976 'the top rock single of all time', says it all: 'How does it feel /To be on your own /With no direction home'.[9]

Few people have pursued the rock 'n' roll dream of freedom as profoundly and persistently as Dylan, but throughout the Sixties and his second great creative period in the mid-Seventies it proved an elusive dream. In this second period, in the albums *Planet Waves, Blood on the Tracks, Desire and Street Legal*, he reflects on the breakdown of human relationships. Particularly he faces up to the impossibility of total autonomous freedom and the fact that we are slaves of sin and shame: 'Heard your songs of freedom and man forever stripped . . . Like a slave in orbit, he's beaten 'til he's tame'.[10]

## The Promised Land

Another of the rock 'n' roll legends who unmistakably demonstrate this longing for freedom is Bruce Springsteen. In the early Seventies he was hailed as 'the new Dylan', but, while not having the profound poetic vision of Dylan, he had his own distinctive contribution to make. He has been very largely responsible for keeping real rock 'n' roll alive through the glam rock and punk rock of the Seventies and early Eighties, and showing that it is still a powerfully expressive medium.

The longing for freedom comes out in songs like 'Independence Day' and 'Hungry Heart' on *The River*, Springsteen's 1980 album. In 'Independence Day' a young man, prodigal-like wants to get away from the restrictions of home. In 'Hungry Heart' a man contemplates the failure of his effort to free himself by leaving his wife and family: 'Ain't nobody like to be alone'.[11]

One of the distinctives of Springsteen's lyrics is the use of biblical imagery to express this longing. In 'Promised Land' from *Darkness on the Edge of Town* he says: 'Mister, I ain't a boy, no, I'm a man /And I believe in a Promised

Land'.[12] In 'Adam Raised a Cain' he even frames the problem in quasi-biblical terms: 'You're born into this life paying /For the sins of somebody else's past'.[13] But although he frames the problems in biblical terms, he has no biblical solutions. There is no Christian hope or freedom from sin. 'My Father's House' on *Nebraska* ends with the statement that 'our sins lie unatoned'.[14]

Another distinctive is the theme of freedom through cars and music. It's really an updating of Chuck Berry on a grander scale. He is conscious of the restrictions and boredom of modern small-town or city life, but the only hope he offers is escape via cars or rock music. Sometimes this escape is proposed as a solution to problems he has outlined in biblical terms, as in 'Racin' in the Street': 'Tonight my baby and me /We're gonna ride into the sea /And wash these sins off our hands'.[15] But he seems to be aware that this is not an adequate response and in *Born in the USA*, one of the great rock 'n' roll albums, there is a pessimism in the title track and in songs like 'Dancing in the Dark'. In the latter he fears the love he craves will be 'just dancing in the dark'.

## Drowned bagpipes and burned fiddles

It is clear from this brief look at the songs of Bob Dylan and Bruce Springsteen that rock music is not all meaningless noise or uninhibited sensuality. It is an area of legitimate human creativity, and one that throws a unique light on the age we live in. There is nothing intrinsically immoral or anti-christian in its form. Indeed, in its best exponents it reveals a longing for freedom, even salvation, which can only be fulfilled in Christ. God has not left himself without witness, and the very musical form has got such longings built into its ancestry. This is not to say that you can pick up any rock record with impunity, any more than you can pick up any newspaper or magazine with impunity. There is gutter rock, just as there is gutter press. The Christian has to be on his guard as he moves through this area, no less than as he moves through life in general.

But there are no grounds for Christian writers and leaders to vilify the whole musical genre, and make people feel guilty about interest in, and concern for, rock music. Christians have, of course, often taken an anti-cultural stance, not least in Presbyterian Scotland where bagpipe-drowning and fiddle-burning was frequently the order of the day when someone was converted. But while I would defend to the death a man's right to drown his own bagpipes or burn his own fiddle (or guitar or record collection) when these were a stumbling-block to him, I must protest in the name of Christian liberty when he demands that his Christian brother drown his bagpipes or burn his fiddle too.

## Solid Rock

There is one other controversial area to be considered. That is the question of whether there can be such a thing as Christian rock music. By 'Christian rock music' I mean rock songs consistent with the Christian world view and written and performed by Christians. (And by 'Christians' I simply mean people who say they believe that Christ died for them. Who am I to judge them any further, when I don't know them?) I believe not only that there can be such a thing as Christian rock music but that it is the very finest there is, because it pursues the highest freedom and it speaks with the greatest urgency. Two examples must suffice - the Christian songs of Bob Dylan and of U2.

Dylan began to express Christian belief and commitment in his songs from 1979 with the release of *Slow Train Coming* and has continued to do so ever since (in spite of constant rumours that he has abandoned Christian faith). The initial reaction of most of the music press was predictably hysterical. 'Dylan as Bible-puncher is just too much to swallow', squealed Chris Bohn in *Melody Maker*.[16] But some, like Charles Shaar Murray in *New Musical Express*, had to admit that Dylan's singing was the best it had ever been. He even goes so far as to say that a verse of 'Precious Angel' 'is some sort of peak in the history of vocal rock and roll'.[17] But the most perceptive and sympathetic treatment came from Paul Williams, who holds the dubious honour of being called 'the father of rock journalism'. His book *Dylan - What Happened?* is a fascinating study in the reaction of a non-Christian to conversion. In writing of Dylan's concerts in late 1979, he too recognised the power of Dylan's Christian rock:

'The fourth of the new songs that demonstrate to me that Christ's Dylan is as bold a creative force as any Dylan we've known is "Hanging on to a Solid Rock" which . . . . just happens to have one of the finer bass-line hooks in the history of rock 'n' roll. . . . Rock 'n' roll has roots in gospel music - in many ways that's where it all started - and this song helps bring things full circle. . . . every moment of the performance pulses with excitement, pulling the audience in like nothing I know of except the last half hour of a Springsteen concert'.[18]

In contrast, Christian writer Steve Turner is rather scathing - 'Instead of taking the themes of exile and escape and extending them toward the conclusion he'd recently arrived at, he set small sermons to music. If you violate the vocabulary of rock 'n' roll, it's as bad as violating the vocabulary of architecture or interior design'.[19] I find this frankly incredible. If rock 'n' roll is about freedom and urgency, what can be more rock 'n' roll than Dylan singing of the insane lawlessness of the world and his liberation from it by Christ, all in a powerful rock-blues idiom?

There is no doubt that in his first post-conversion albums, *Slow Train Coming* and *Saved*, Dylan was urgently communicating the fact that the world and his own life were in a mess and that Christ was the only answer. What aroused most journalistic ire at the time was the reappearance of moral and political judgements in his songs as in 'Slow Train': 'People starving and thirsting, grain elevators are bursting . . . . They say lose your inhibitions, follow your own ambitions'.[20]

What the journalists failed to recognise was that now, in contrast to his protest period, Dylan had discovered there is a basis in God's absolutes for making moral judgements - 'There's only one authority and that's the authority on high'.[21] But what about the great rock 'n' roll theme of freedom? How does Dylan conceive of it now? He sees it as attainable only through Christ: 'He bought me with a price, Freed me from the pit'.[22]

He also recognises that autonomous freedom is impossible. No one can be a law to himself - 'You're gonna have to serve somebody /It may be the devil or it may be the Lord'.[23] True freedom can only be achieved through serving Jesus Christ. But he never gives the impression that he has achieved complete freedom. He's still 'pressing on'. He's still longing for the completed freedom of 'a kingdom they call Heaven /A place where there is no pain of birth'[24] and for the return of Christ, which is made the basis of an appeal to yield to Christ in the beautiful 'When He Returns': 'Surrender your crown on this bloodstained ground, take off your mask, /He sees your deeds, He knows your needs even before you ask'.[25]

Dylan has gone on from these early beginnings to write some extraordinarily powerful and beautiful songs looking at many areas of life from a Christian point of view, but not necessarily mentioning Jesus in every verse (which is what his critics seem to expect a Christian artist to do - they should try reading *Out of the Silent Planet* by C.S. Lewis). The response of his critics was again predictable. When he sang clear statements of Christian faith they said: This is propaganda; when he reformed his own particular style of poetic imagery, they said: He has abandoned Christianity. He can't win. In many of these later songs he speaks honestly of the struggles and longings of Christian experience, as in 'I and I', 'Dark Eyes' and especially 'Every Grain of Sand': 'I gaze into the doorway of temptation's angry flame /And every time I pass that way I always hear my name'.[26]

In particular Dylan appears to be a firm believer in the doctrine of Christian liberty. *Trust yourself* has been misunderstood as recommending trust in oneself as opposed to trust in God. In reality it is advising us to trust our own judgement rather than that of others. It is a restatement of the Protestant 'right of private judgement': 'Don't put your hope in ungodly man /Or be a slave to what somebody else believes'.[27]

I am aware that all kinds of rumours have been circulated about Dylan's abandoning Christianity (sometimes allegedly in favour of a return to his native Judaism), but he has given no indication of this in his albums or his concerts. On the contrary, on the *Knocked Out Loaded* album he sings without embarrassment the Kris Kristofferson song 'They Killed Him' in which Christ is set on a wholly different level from other 'heroes' like Gandhi and Martin Luther King - 'The only Son of God Almighty, the only One called Jesus Christ'. No Judaistic Jew could sing that - only a Messianic one. But even if Dylan did backslide or even become apostate, that could never uncreate his Christian songs which prove that it is possible to make rock music of the highest order which expresses the Christian world view.

## *You loosed the chains*

The Irish band U2 came to articulate a Christian voice in rock from a very different background from Bob Dylan. For a start most of them were hardly five years old when Dylan was redirecting rock music in 1965. But their lead singer Bono recognises Dylan as one of the artists who have inspired him. And U2's music has a similar quality to Dylan's. It is glorious rock music in which the lyrics are extremely important.

In March 1985 *Rolling Stone* named U2 as the 'Band of the '80s'. In 1987, U2 were featured on the cover of the April issue of *Time* magazine, only the third rock 'n' roll band to receive such an accolade, the other two being the Beatles and The Who. Two singles from their 1987 album, *The Joshua Tree*, reached No. 1 in the States. One of these, 'I Still Haven't Found What I'm Looking For', has been described by Steve Turner as possibly 'the ultimate rock 'n' roll redemptive song': 'You broke the bonds /You loosed the chains /You carried the cross /And my shame'.[28] One of the strengths of this powerful song is that, as well as affirming faith in the redemptive death of Christ, it still expresses that longing for ultimate freedom which is common to both Christianity and rock 'n' roll, but which will only be fulfilled in the realisation of the Christian hope.

Interestingly, much of what I've been trying to say in this chapter comes together in a couple of songs on the 1988 U2 album *Rattle and Hum*, released during the final stages of putting this book together. In 'Love Rescue Me', written and performed by Bob Dylan and Bono of U2, there is a clear recognition that we need to be rescued, liberated. But one verse has been misunderstood as a rejection of Christianity. After quoting from Psalm 23 ('Yea though I walk through the valley of the shadow . . . . I will fear no evil') they continue: 'I have cursed thy rod and staff /They no longer comfort me'.[29]

This is the kind of thing that is quoted to 'prove' that Dylan and Bono are no longer Christians. But this is to misunderstand the structure of the song. Each verse describes a situation from which the singer wishes to be liberated, ending with the words 'Love rescue me'. He is lamenting the fact that the rod and staff no longer comfort him. He recognises that he needs to be rescued from this condition. The critics also fail to realise that Christians have to face up to a sense of sin and failure. They think that Christians should be 'sugar and spice and all things nice' and are phased when they are not. I recommend they read the Book of Psalms.

That Bono is in no way rejecting Christianity is clearly seen in the very next song, 'When Love Comes to Town' performed with B.B. King, the legendary R & B guitarist. In traditional Gospel music style, Bono recognises his sinful solidarity with those who crucified Jesus: 'I threw the dice when they pierced his side /But I've seen love conquer the great divide'.[30]

In bringing rock music back to its roots in Gospel,

country and R & B, Dylan and U2 have shown it to be a
powerful instrument for communicating the Christian
world view in general and the Christian theme of freedom
in particular.

CHAPTER 12
# FUTURE FREEDOM

Nothing characterises the twentieth century more than fear of the future. There are fears concerning the abuse of technology and biological engineering, the pollution and destruction of the environment, and above all the nuclear threat. As we near the end of the second millenium, books about the future have been almost consistently pessimistic - Aldous Huxley's *Brave New World*, George Orwell's *1984*, Antony Burgess' *A Clockwork Orange*. There is also a persistent feeling of hopelessness at the individual level. In the title track of *Born in the USA*, the album that sums up the post-Vietnam generation of young Americans in the eighties, Bruce Springsteen sings:

*I'm ten years burning down the road*
*Nowhere to run, aint got nowhere to go.*[1]

The words of the Apostle Paul describing the fears and emptiness of the post-Augustan Roman world are equally true of the modern age - 'without hope and without God in the world' (Ephesians 2:12).

## *Without Hope*

This pessimism manifests itself at two levels - fear about the future of the human race, and loss of hope in life after death. Since World War II there has been a steady acceleration of pessimism concerning mankind in general. H.G. Wells, so well known in the first half of the century for his optimistic constructions of the future, ended his life in despair. In 1945, in *Mind at the End of its Tether* he wrote, 'Homo sapiens, as he has been pleased to call himself, is played out'. Twenty years later Bob Dylan sang Desolation Row, a catalogue of the absurdities of modern life:

*Praise be to Nero's Neptune the Titanic sails at dawn*
*And everybody's shouting 'Which side are you on?'*[2]

The Titanic, built as the unsinkable ship and sinking on its

maiden voyage with tragic loss of life, stands as an elo-
quent symbol of naive faith in the inevitability of human
progress and of the total destruction that may lurk over
the horizon of the future.

Of course, not all attitudes to the future are pessimistic.
Marxism, in all its many forms, remains one of the most
utopian political philosophies of our time. The revolution
of the proletariat, given time, will produce the utopia of
the classless society. But is such doctrinaire optimism justified by the evidence? Arthur Koestler's novel *Darkness
at Noon* was based on the experience of the Moscow
Trials in the thirties. The book ends with the thoughts of
Rubashov, the main character, who has been condemned
to death for crimes against the state and who now awaits
his final summons:

> What happened to those masses, to this people? For
> forty years it had been driven through the desert, with
> threats and promises, with imaginary terrors and imagi-
> nary rewards. But where the Promised Land? Did there
> really exist any such goal for this wandering mankind?
> That was a question to which he would have liked an
> answer before it was too late. Moses had not been
> allowed to enter the land of promise either. But he had
> been allowed to see it from the top of the mountain,
> spread at his feet. Thus it was easy to die with the visi-
> ble certainty of one's goal before one's eyes. He,
> Nicolai Salmanowitch Rubashov, had not been taken
> to the top of a mountain; and wherever his eye looked,
> he saw nothing but desert and the darkness of night.[3]

If there is no life beyond death and this life provides nothing but blind, empty optimism, then the light in us is darkness indeed. And is not this the fear above all others that
haunts modern man - the fear of death? If the nineteenth
century tried to conceal the facts of life, the twentieth has
tried to conceal the facts of death. Woody Allen, the film-
director and comedian, encapsulated the modern attitude
in his own inimitable style: 'It's not that I'm afraid to die, I
just don't want to be there when it happens'.[4] The ancient
Egyptian obsession with preserving the dead body from

decay has returned with a vengeance in the neo-pagan West, where everything possible is done to cushion the bereaved from the harsh reality of death. It is a cruel kindness. On the other hand, cremation can be seen as a blunt statement that death is the end.

Impersonalism has done everything it can to remove the fear of death by emphasising that there is nothing to fear beyond death because there is nothing beyond death. But when fear moves out, despair moves in. This despair has been most nobly exemplified by the philosopher Bertrand Russell:

> 'Brief and powerless is man's life; on him and all his race the slow, sure doom falls pitiless and dark. Blind to good and evil, reckless of destruction, omnipotent matter rolls on its relentless way; for man, condemned today to lose his dearest, tomorrow himself to pass through the gate of darkness, it remains only to cherish, ere yet the blow fall, the lofty thoughts that ennoble his little day . . . .'[5]

Noble and stoic it may be, but it is bleak despair none-the-less. In similar vein, but altogether more poignant is Elegy by Dylan Thomas, written not long before his death. These are the last lines:

> *Out of his eyes I saw the last light glide.*
> *Here among the light of the lording sky*
> *An old blind man is with me where I go*
> *Walking in the meadow of his son's eye*
> *On whom a world of ills came down like snow.*
> *He cried as he died, fearing at last the sphere's*
> *Last sound, the world going out without a breath:*
> *Too proud to cry, too frail to check the tears,*
> *And caught between two nights, blindness and death.*
> *O deepest wound of all that he should die*
> *On that darkest day. Oh he could hide*
> *The tears out of his eyes, too proud to cry.*
> *Until I die he will not leave my side.*[6]

As Francis Schaeffer says in *The God who is There*, 'This is sensitivity crying out in darkness'.[7] If it doesn't make you weep, nothing will. If you believe in Russell's 'omnipotent matter', you will weep in despair. If you know the Christian hope, you will weep with compassion.

## Christ Jesus our Hope

The first century Roman world, to which the Apostle Paul proclaimed the good news of Jesus, was not all that unlike our own. Catullus spoke for the majority when he said, 'Suns may set and rise again. When once our brief light has set, one unbroken night remains'. Into this bleak, grey world the gospel broke like the dawn. Hope is an essential element of the gospel. Paul even spoke of Jesus as 'Christ Jesus our hope' (1 Timothy 1:1).

How is Christ Jesus our hope? First of all he is our hope because, with his authority as the Son of God, he assures us of the eternal existence of the human person. In concluding his parable of the last judgement, he says, 'Then they will go away to eternal punishment, but the righteous to eternal life' (Matthew 25:46). As well as clearly teaching, as we shall see, that there are two distinct destinations beyond death, heaven and hell, Jesus makes it as plain as language can that human beings are eternal. Death is not the end, as Dylan says in a recent song: 'When you're sad and when you're lonely and you haven't got a friend /Just remember that death is not the end'.[8]

C.S. Lewis in *The Weight of Glory* shows something of what this means for our present attitude to each other:

'It is a serious thing to live in a society of possible gods and goddesses, to remember that the dullest and most uninteresting person you can talk to may one day be a creature which, if you saw it now, you would be strongly tempted to worship, or else a horror and a corruption such as you now meet, if at all, only in a nightmare. All day long we are, in some degree, helping each other to one or other of these destinations. It is in the light of these overwhelming possibilities, it is with the awe and circumspection proper to them, that we should conduct all our dealings with one another, all friendships, all loves, all play, all politics. There are no ordinary people. You have never talked to a mere mortal. Nations, cultures, arts, civilisations - these are mortal, and their life is to ours as the life of a gnat. But it is immortals whom we joke with, work with, marry, snub and exploit - immortal horrors or everlasting splendours'.[9]

However, this teaching of Jesus' not only provides the basis for hope, it also intensifies the trauma of death. There are two eternal conditions, eternal punishment and eternal life. Or, as C.S. Lewis puts it, we are immortals, but immortal horrors or everlasting splendours. To make matters worse, the Bible makes it abundantly plain that we all deserve hell. 'The wages of sin is death', says the Apostle Paul (Romans 6:23). 'Everyone who sins is a slave to sin', says Jesus (John 8:34). So unless we are freed, we are on the road to hell. Amazingly, all but four of the twenty-two uses of the words translated 'hell' in the New Testament are on the lips of Jesus. In addition he does not mince his words in describing hell. It is 'eternal punishment' (Matthew 25:46), it is being 'in torment' (Luke 16:23), it is where 'their worm does not die, and the fire is not quenched' (Mark 9:48). How is this type of language compatable with Jesus' being the God of love? But does not love warn of danger and teach the way of escape? Is not this what Jesus does lovingly and seriously? And then there is also the necessity of hell. Again it is C.S. Lewis that puts his finger on it, this time in *The Great Divorce*:

'Either the day must come when joy prevails and all the makers of misery are no longer able to infect it: or else for ever and ever the makers of misery can destroy in others the happiness they reject for themselves. I know it has a grand sound to say that ye'll accept no salvation which leaves even one creature in the dark outside. But watch that sophistry or ye'll make a Dog in a Manger the tyrant of the universe'.[10]

In a strange way, hell is the final confirmation of the significance and dignity of man. God must punish sin and exclude evil from his new universe. But he will not break man or unmake him. He allows man to stand in his rebellion. He confirms his choice. That is hell's necessity and its horror.

## The Disarming of Death

The Christian message of hope for the individual is that death is not the end and that there is a way of escape from hell. That way of escape is through the atoning death of Jesus Christ in the place of sinners, as we saw in chapter 9. That is why Paul can proclaim victory over death:

> 'Where, O death, is your victory? Where, O death, is your sting? The sting of death is sin, and the power of sin is the law. But thanks be to God! He gives us the victory through our Lord Jesus Christ' (1 Corinthians 15:55-57).

This confident hope of victory over death has probably nowhere in all of literature been better illustrated than by Mr. Valiant-for-Truth in John Bunyan's *Pilgrim's Progress*:

> 'Then said he, "I am going to my fathers, and though with great difficulty I am got hither, yet now I do not repent me of all the trouble I have been at to arrive where I am. My sword, I give to him that shall succeed me in my pilgrimage, and my courage and skill to him that can get it. My marks and scars I carry with me, to be a witness for me that I have fought his battles who will now be my rewarder". When the day that he must go hence was come, many accompanied him to the river side, unto which as he went he said, "Death, where is thy sting?" And as he went down deeper he said, "Grave, where is thy victory?" So he passed over and the trumpets sounded for him on the other side'.[11]

## Death reversed

Marvellous though that is, this is not the final realisation of the Christian hope. There is more to come! Not only has Christ died for our sins, but he rose again on the third day

(1 Corinthians 15:3,4). For the Apostle Paul this is the indispensable heart of Christianity. 'And if Christ has not been raised, our preaching is useless and so is your faith . . . . If only for this life we have hope in Christ, we are to be pitied more than all men. But Christ has indeed been raised from the dead, the firstfruits of those who have fallen asleep'(1 Corinthians 15:14,19,20). In other words, not only has Christ disarmed death, he has reversed it too.

This is one thing that many contemporary theologians, with their rejection of the supernatural, cannot accept. But then they make their irrational leap of faith and say, 'It doesn't matter if the body of Jesus is still mouldering in some Jerusalem grave. His spirit is still alive!' Unfortunately, this is indistinguishable from the pietistic cliches of some evangelicals - 'You ask me how I know he lives. He lives within my heart'. How different from the New Testament! The very Greek word used by the New Testament writers for resurrection - *anastasis* - means bodily (not spiritual) resurrection. This was what was unacceptable about the gospel to the Greeks. 'When they heard about the resurrection of the dead, some of them sneered . . . .' (Acts 17:32). This took place in Athens as Paul was explaining the gospel to the venerable Council of the Areopagus. At the founding of the Areopagus, as portrayed by Aeschylus, the god Apollo says,'Once a man dies and the earth drinks up his blood, there is no resurrection'.[12] There is no doubt that the Apostle could have made the gospel much more palatable to the Greeks if he had removed all reference to the resurrection. But he could not, simply because that would have been a lie. The fact was that the tomb was empty on the third day and the risen Jesus had been seen by many eye-witnesses, including Paul himself.

Many attempts have been made to explain away the resurrection of Jesus, but they have all foundered on the rock of the evidence, and particularly the fact of the empty tomb. One of the most celebrated of these attempts was made by Frank Morison. He set out to write a book proving that the story of the resurrection was nothing but a fairy tale ending to the truly noble history of Jesus of Nazareth. After he had examined the evidence and he came to write the book, he had to entitle the first chapter 'The Book that Refused to be Written'. He had been convinced by the evidence that Jesus actually did rise from the dead.[13]

This is not just a matter of past history. If Christ has conquered death, then he has done so for all who trust in him. His resurrection guarrantees our resurrection. The day will come when all the physical miseries as well as the psychological miseries of this life will be no more. 'He will wipe every tear from their eyes. There will be no more death or mourning or crying or pain, for the old order of things has passed away' (Revelation 21:4). Joni Eareckson came to a living faith in Jesus Christ through heart-rending struggles after being paralysed in a diving accident. She has been a quadriplegic ever since. She knows what the resurrection day will mean for her - 'I'll be on my feet dancing'.[14]

## Hope in the World

Is the Christian hope only a personal, individual hope? Has it nothing to say about the history of the world, about mankind in general, about the world and the problems of the world? Is it just 'pie in the sky when you die'? Absolutely not! For one thing, our hope is not heaven or the resurrection in themselves. Our hope is Christ Jesus himself. It is because he is who he is and because he has done what he has done that we have the hope of heaven and the resurrection. But he is the hope not just at the individual level but at the cosmic level too. The Christian does not despair of the world in its present condition because Christ is in control. He is the King of kings. In that marvellous vision given to John, he is the Lamb at the centre of the throne, the throne from which the universe is governed. He it is who implements the will of God in the world (Revelation 5:6, 6:1). God the Father has 'placed all things under his feet and appointed him to be head over everything for the church' (Ephesians 1:22).

Therefore, the Christian need fear no evil, not only as he passes through the valley of the shadow of death, but also as he passes through this world. And he can have this confidence not only for himself, but also for the whole church of Jesus Christ. The church is founded upon the rock Christ Jesus and the gates of hell will not prevail against it (Matthew 16:18). The world will not be destroyed by evil. It will not be laid waste by a demonic technocracy, nor annihilated by a nuclear cataclysm. There are glorious promises, yet to be fulfilled, of the gospel being preached to every nation, of the conversion of Israel bringing riches to the world and of Christ bringing the present history of the world to an end when he returns (Matthew 24:14, Romans 11:11,12, Matthew 24:37-39).

And there is something more. Christ Jesus is our hope in that he gives us work to do. Often our hopelessness and our helplessness go hand in hand. Our fear of the future freezes us into inactivity. We don't know what the future holds. We don't know what to do. And we don't know if it's worth doing anything anyway. Having Christ Jesus as our hope changes all that. He commands us to pray that the kingdom of God may come, that God's will may be done on earth as it is in heaven (Matthew 6:10). He says we must work while we have the day of opportunity (John 9:4). Through his apostle he tells us to glorify God in our bodies (1 Corinthians 6:20).

This spirit of those who have been freed from a fear of the future and who have a hope of glorifying God on earth was exemplified by the old Covenanter, Donald Cargill. A minister who had accepted the king's authority over the church had remarked about Cargill's obstinate adherance to the headship of Christ alone over his church, 'What needs all this ado? We will get heaven, and they will get no more'. When this was reported to Cargill, his reply was noble and profound: 'Yes, we will get more; we will get God glorified on earth, which is more than heaven'.[15]

# REFERENCES

## PART 1: Life

### *Chapter 1: The Human Image*

1.    Fred Hoyle, *The Nature of the Universe*, Penguin 1960, pp. 120-21
2.    B.F. Skinner, *Beyond Freedom and Dignity*, New York: Knopf, 1971, p. 202
3.    Jacques Monod, *Chance and Necessity*, New York: Knopf, 1971, p.145
4.    Quoted by C.S. Lewis, *Miracles*, Collins Fontana, 1974, p. 19
5.    *ibid.* p. 22
6.    *The Didache* and Josephus, *Contra Apion* 2.202, *Antiquities* 4.277

### *Chapter 2: Life in Our Hands*

1.    *Report of the Committee of Inquiry into Human Fertilisation and Embryology*, Her Majesty's Stationery Office, 1984, p. 20, 23-24
2.    *ibid.* p. 47
3.    C.S. Lewis, *The Abolition of Man*, Collins, 1978; *That Hideous Strength*, Pan, 1979

### *Chapter 3: Force and Violence*

1.    Albert Camus, *The Plague*, Penguin, 1969
2.    Arthur Koestler, *The Ghost in the Machine*, Hutchinson, 1967, p.267
3.    *ibid.* p.339
4.    Konrad Lorenz, *On Aggression*, New York: Bantam, 1967
5.    Quoted by Francis Schaeffer, *How Should We Then Live?*, New Jersey: Fleming H. Revell, 1976, p. 217
6.    Fyodor Dostoyevsky, *The Brothers Karamazov*, translated by Constance Garnett, The Modern Library, New York, p. 297
7.    Quoted by Os Guinness in *The Dust of Death*, IVP, 1973, p. 163
8.    C.E.M. Joad, *The Recovery of Belief*, Faber, 1952, p. 82
9.    John Steinbeck, *East of Eden*, New York: Viking, 1952, p. 226
10.    Stuart Barton Babbage, *The Mark of Cain*, Paternoster Press, 1966, pp. 9,10
11.    Francis Schaeffer, *The God Who is There*, Hodder and Stoughton, 1968, pp. 101, 107

### *Chapter 4: The Peace Movement*

1.    C.S. Lewis, 'Blimpophobia', in *Present Concerns* (ed. Walter Hooper), Collins, 1986, p. 42

2.      Martin Luther King, *Stride Toward Freedom*, New York: Harper, 1958, p.224
3.      Bob Dylan, 'Masters of War', *Lyrics 1962-1985*, Jonathan Cape, p. 56
4.      C.S. Lewis, 'On Living in an Atomic Age'; *in Present Concerns*, p. 73ff
5.      Bertrand Russell, 'A Free Man's Worship' in *Why I am Not a Christian*, Simon and Shuster, 1966, p. 107
6.      Jim Wallis, *Call to Conversion*, Lion, 1982
7.      Ronald Sider and Richard K. Taylor, *Nuclear Holocaust and Christian Hope*, Hodder and Stoughton, 1982, p. 145

## PART 2: Love

### Chapter 5: Love Minus Zero

1.      C.S. Lewis, *Mere Christianity*, Collins, 1955, p.52
2.      Leonard Cohen,' Story of Isaac', *Songs from a Room*, CBS, 1968
3.      C.S. Lewis, *The Lion, the Witch and the Wardrobe*, Penguin, 1959, p. 129
4.      *The Trial of Lady Chatterley*, ed. C.H. Rolph, Penguin, 1961, p. 160

### Chapter 6: The Power of Love

1.      J.R.R. Tolkien, *The Silmarillion*, Unwin Paperbacks, 1983, p. 58
2.      C.S.Lewis, *The Four Loves*, Collins, 1963, p. 93
3.      Quoted by Stuart Barton Babbage *ibid.* p. 131
4.      C.S. Lewis, *ibid.* p.94
5.      John White, *Eros Defiled*, IVP, 1977, p. 24
6.      *The Power of Love*, CBS, 1985

### Chapter 8: Throwaway Relationships

1.      Quoted by Os Guinness, *The Gravedigger File*, Hodder and Stoughton, 1983, p. 102
2.      John White, *ibid.* p. 81
3.      Quoted by Stuart Barton Babbage, *ibid.* p.139
4.      Bob Dylan, 'Chimes of Freedom', *Lyrics 1962-1985*, Jonathan Cape, p.133
5.      Os Guinness, *ibid.* p. 101, 102
6.      *ibid.* p. 103
7.      John Murray, *Divorce*, Presbyterian and Reformed Publishing Co., 1961, p. 43
8.      ibid. p. 76
9.      Westminster Confession of Faith XXIV, VI
10.     *See Marriage and Divorce: A Report of the Study Panel of the Free Church of Scotland*, 1988, pp. 29-30

## PART 3: Liberty

### *Chapter 9: Christian Liberation*

1. Robert Burns, *Scots Wha Hae*
2. Leonard Cohen, 'Bird on the Wir'e, *Songs From a Room*, CBS, 1968
3. Albert Camus, *The Fall*, Penguin, 1963, p. 80
4. Tacitus, *History*, 5.9

### *Chapter 10: Freedom from Addiction*

1. C.S. Lewis, *The Abolition of Man*, Collins, 1978, p. 20
2. Johnny Cash, *Man in Black*, Hodder and Stoughton, 1975

### *Chapter 11: Chimes of Freedom*

1. John Blanchard, *Pop Goes The Gospel*, Evangelical Press, 1983
2. Steve Turner, H*ungry for Heaven*, Kingsway, 1988, pp. 156-57
3. *ibid*. p. 32
4. *Encyclopedia of Rock*, Octopus, 1983, pp. 55-6
5. Bob Dylan, 'Blowin' in the Wind', *Lyrics 1962-1985*, Jonathan Cape, p.53
6. Bob Dylan, 'Chimes of Freedom', *Lyrics 1962-1985*, Jonathan Cape, p.132
7. Bob Dylan, 'My Back Pages', *Lyrics 1962-1985*, Jonathan Cape, p.139
8. Bob Dylan, 'Stuck Inside of Mobile with the Memphis Blues Again', *Lyrics 1962-1985*. Jonathan Cape, p. 229
9. Bob Dylan, 'Like a Rolling Stone',*Lyrics 1962-1985*, Jonathan Cape, p.191
10. Bob Dylan, 'Dirge', *Lyrics 1962-1985*, Jonathan Cape, p.347
11. Bruce Springsteen, 'Hungry Heart', *The River*, CBS 1980
12. Bruce Springsteen, 'Promised Land', *Darkness on the Edge of Town*, CBS 1978
13. Bruce Springsteen, 'Adam Raised a Cain', *Darkness on the Edge of Town*, CBS 1978
14. Bruce Springsteen, 'My Father's House', *Nebraska*, CBS 1982
15. Bruce Springsteen, 'Racin' in the Street', *Darkness on the Edge of Town*, CBS 1978
16. *Melody Maker*, 25th August 1979, p. 25
17. *New Musical Express*, 25th August 1979, p. 36
18. Paul Williams, *Dylan - What Happened?*, and books/Entwhistle Books, 1979, p. 107
19. Steve Turner, *ibid*., p. 27
20. Bob Dylan, 'Slow Train', *Lyrics 1962-1985*, Jonathan Cape, p.436
21. Bob Dylan, 'Gonna Change My Way of Thinking', *Lyrics 1962-1985*, Jonathan Cape, p.428
22. Bob Dylan, 'Saved', *Lyrics 1962-1985*, Jonathan Cape, p.443

23.     Bob Dylan, 'Gotta Serve Somebody', *Lyrics 1962-1985,* Jonathan Cape, p.423
24.     Bob Dylan, 'Gonna Change My Way of Thinking', *Lyrics 1962-1985,* Jonathan Cape, p.429
25.     Bob Dylan, 'When He Returns', *Lyrics 1962-1985,* Jonathan Cape, p.437
26.     Bob Dylan, 'Every Grain of Sand', *Lyrics 1962-1985,* Jonathan Cape, p.462
27.     Bob Dylan, 'Trust Yourself', *Lyrics 1962-1985,* Jonathan Cape, p. 495
28.     U2, 'I Still Haven't Found What I'm Looking For', *The Joshua Tree,* Island, 1987
29.     U2, 'Love Rescue Me', *Rattle and Hum,* Island, 1988
30.     U2 'When Love Comes To Town', *Rattle and Hum,* Island, 1988

## Chapter 12: Future Freedom

1.      Bruce Springsteen, *Born in the USA,* CBS, 1984
2.      Bob Dylan, 'Desolation Row', *Lyrics 1962-1985,* Jonathan Cape, p.206
3.      Arthur Koestler, *Darkness at Noon,* Jonathan Cape, 1940, pp. 253-54
4.      Woody Allen, 'Death (a play)'; in *Without Feathers,* 1972
5.      Bertrand Russell, 'A Free Man's Worship'; in *Why I am Not a Christian,* Simon and Shuster, 1966, pp. 115-16
6.      Dylan Thomas, *Collected Poems,* 1934-52, J.M. Dent and Sons, London, 1959, pp. 179-80
7.      Francis Schaeffer, *The God Who Is There,* Hodder and Stoughton, 1968, p. 41
8.      Bob Dylan, 'Death is not the end', *Down in the Groove,* CBS 1988
9.      C.S. Lewis, 'The Weight of Glory'; in *Screwtape Proposes a Toast,* Collins, 1965, p. 109
10.     C.S. Lewis, *The Great Divorce,* Collins, 1972, p. 111
11.     John Bunyan, *The Pilgrim's Progress,* Henry Bohn, London, 1857, p. 463
12.     Aeschylus, *Eumenides,* 647
13.     Frank Morison, *Who Moved the Stone?,* Faber and Faber, 1930
14.     Joni Earickson, *Joni and A Step Further,* Pickering and Inglis, 1978 and 1979
15.     Alexander Smellie, *Men of the Covenant,* Andrew Melrose, London, 1904, p. 283